Secret Message
Bible
Word Searches

D0448437

BARBOUR
PUBLISHING

2009

Puzzles designed by Annie Tipton, John Hudson Tiner, Kelly Williams, Paul Muckley, and Rebecca Germany.

ISBN 978-1-60260-349-3

All scripture quotations are taken from the King James Version of the Bible.

Published by Barbour Publishing, Inc., P.O. Box 719, Uhrichsville, Ohio 44683, www.barbourbooks.com

Our mission is to publish and distribute inspirational products offering exceptional value and biblical encouragement to the masses.

eepa Member of the
Evangelical Christian
Publishers Association

Printed in the United States of America.

Welcome to
Secret Message
Bible Word Search!

If you like Bible word searches, you'll love this book. Here are 101 brand-new puzzles to expand your Bible knowledge and test your word search skills, as thousands of search words— each one selected from the King James Version of the Bible— await your discovery. And there's a bonus: In each puzzle the leftover letters spell out a trivia question to challenge your memory of the scripture!

Each puzzle features a scripture passage with the search words printed in **bold type**. When a phrase is **bold and underlined**, those words will be found together in the puzzle grid. Once you've found all the search words, begin at the top left-hand corner of the puzzle and read the leftover letters in order—they'll spell out the trivia question that adds to the fun. If you run into the letter "X" repeated, the question is complete. Answers—for both the puzzles and the trivia questions—appear at the back of the book.

We know you're eager to get started, so just one final word: Enjoy!

1

Trouble between Brothers

Genesis 4:6–10

And the Lord said unto Cain, Why art thou wroth? and why is thy countenance fallen? If thou doest well, shalt thou not be accepted? and if thou doest not well, sin lieth at the door. And unto thee shall be his desire, and thou shalt rule over him. And Cain talked with Abel his brother: and it came to pass, when they were in the field, that Cain rose up against Abel his brother, and slew him. And the Lord said unto Cain, Where is Abel thy brother? And he said, I know not: Am I my brother's keeper? And he said, What hast thou done? the voice of thy brother's blood crieth unto me from the ground.

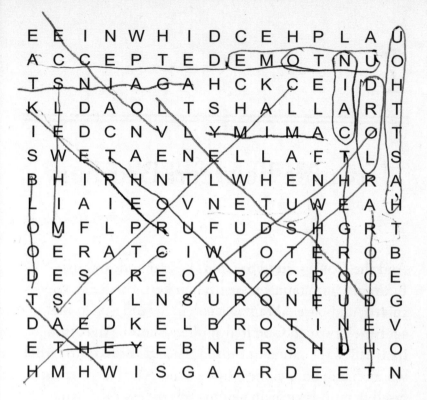

```
E E I N W H I D C E H P L A U
A C C E P T E D E M O T N U O
T S N I A G A H C K C E I D H
K L D A O L T S H A L L A R T
I E D C N V L Y M I M A C O S
S W E T A E N E L L A F T L A
B H I R H N T L W H E N H R A
L I A I E O V N E T U W E A H
O M F L P R U F U D S H G R T
O E R A T C I W I O T E R O B
D E S I R E O A R O C R O O E
T S I I L N S U R O N E U D G
D A E D K E L B R O T I N E V
E T H E Y E B N F R S N D H O
H M H W I S G A A R D E E T N
```

Secret Message

_____

_____

_____

_____

_____

_____

2

Sarah's Laughter

Genesis 21:1–6

And the **LORD visited Sarah** as he had said, and the LORD did unto Sarah as he had **spoken**. For Sarah **conceived**, and **bare** Abraham a **son** in his **old age**, at the **set time** of which **God had spoken** to him. And **Abraham** called the **name** of his son that was **born** unto him, whom Sarah bare to him, **Isaac**. And Abraham **circumcised** his son Isaac being **eight** days old, as God had **commanded** him. And Abraham was an **hundred** years old, when his son Isaac was born unto him. And Sarah said, God **hath made** me to **laugh**, **so that** all that **hear** will laugh **with me**.

W H G U A L H E R C E D I S D
V H A T H M A D E O N G P W O
I D C O D M M A N N E O A I D
S D A B O R N B R C K A B T E
I E G A D L O H A E O M R H S
T M C T O D T L N I P A A M I
E I O K E I E S O V S S H E C
D T M H E A R R S E D E A A M
A C M A N D E T D D A T M H U
E N A O F M F E R N H H I M C
H A N C A A S I S A U T B U R
A R D N N T O F F E R H I N I
R G E X X M A D D V I G A B C
A E D T A H T O S A B I R I C
S O H P Q U G S D A H E R A B

Secret Message

_____

_____

_____

_____

_____

_____

3

Promise to Abraham

Genesis 22:15–18

And **the angel** of the **LORD called unto Abraham** out of **heaven** the **second time**, **and said**, By **myself** have I **sworn**, saith the LORD, for **because thou hast done this thing**, and hast not **withheld** thy son, **thine only son**: That in **blessing** I will bless thee, and in **multiplying** I will multiply **thy seed** as the **stars** of the heaven, and as the **sand** which is upon the **sea shore**; and thy seed **shall possess** the **gate** of **his enemies**; and in thy seed shall **all the nations** of the **earth** be **blessed**; because thou hast **obeyed my voice**.

```
E N I H T C M A H A R B A W H
O E R O H S A E S G W A L S T
H D E M O E R L S M N S L O N
B E C A U S E A L E Y I T T H
L E I A H L T A T E C S H B O
E S O R A S T H S S D O E T A
S Y V H S H E I D A A O N L M
S H Y D T A H I P D N U A D F
E T M R N T A P M L D D T I D
D N A G E S O O Y E Y R I T N
W E E N D I B S T H N I O H E
G L O N H E O S O H L E N L V
A D A D Y N F E R T O M S G A
T I M E B L E S S I N G G I E
E O D L L A H S S W O R N D H
```

Secret Message

ISAAC

4

Baby in an Ark

Exodus 2:1–5

And there went **a man of** the **house of Levi**, and took to **wife** a **daughter** of Levi. And the **woman conceived**, and **bare a son**: and when **she saw him** that he was a **goodly child**, she hid him **three months**. And when she could not **longer hide** him, she took for him an **ark of bulrushes**, and **daubed** it with **slime** and **with pitch**, and put the child **therein**; and she laid it in the **flags** by the **river's brink**. And his **sister stood afar off**, to wit what would be **done to him**. And the daughter of **Pharaoh** came down to **wash herself** at the river; and her **maidens walked** along by the **river's side**; and when she saw the ark among the flags, she sent her maid **to fetch** it.

```
F N W H D A U G H T E R T S O
L A F D R E I D R E P H E H R
A M F A R I V A I O R H H E S
G O O D L Y V I V E S S T D A
S W R U G H V E E U F S E H T
P D A U B E D M R C I I O L O
T H F E L I O L S S N U W N F
S C A F H N U H B R S O P O E
L T O R T B E A R E L I C S T
I I O H A S Y A I T O O D A C
M P S O A O W M N N N U D E H
E H R W D S H A K E G T L R H
E T H E R E I N S N E D I A M
M H O T E N O D H R B H B A
M W A L K E D F O K R A C B Y
```

Secret Message

Moses

5

Food from Heaven

Exodus 16:2–4

And the whole **congregation** of the **children** of **Israel murmured** against **Moses** and **Aaron** in the **wilderness**: And the children of Israel **said unto** them, **Would to God** we **had died by the hand** of the LORD in the **land of Egypt**, when we sat by the **flesh pots**, and when we did **eat bread** to **the full**; for ye have **brought** us **forth** into this wilderness, to **kill this** whole **assembly** with **hunger**. Then said the LORD unto Moses, Behold, **I will rain** bread from **heaven** for you; and the **people** shall go out and **gather** a certain **rate every day**, that I may **prove** them, **whether** they **will walk** in **my law**, or no.

```
W W I L L W A L K H A T L F C
E V O R P A O M O U N T A O O
V D E R U M R U M F F H N R F
E A A S S E M B L Y A G D T O
R E H T E H W E O D R D O H S
Y R W H T D S A D E T S F S G
D B A G T H N I G H R O E P N
A T M U P I E A H E E N G E E
Y A R O S D T F H T R E Y O R
D E T R S I R T U E L A P P D
W S A B O E A N D L H L I L L
A E O N G G S L O N L T I E I
L O T N U D I A S R T H Y K H
Y E U S I W I L L R A I N B C
M H E A V E N I X T H A D A Y
```

Secret Message

Mana

_____

_____

_____

_____

_____

_____

6

Year of Liberty

Leviticus 25:10–13

And ye shall **hallow** the **fiftieth year**, and **proclaim liberty throughout** all the land unto all the **inhabitants thereof**: it shall be a jubile unto you; and ye shall **return every man** unto his **possession**, and ye shall return every man unto his **family**. A jubile shall **that** fiftieth year be unto you: ye shall not sow, **neither reap** that **which groweth** of **itself** in it, nor gather the **grapes** in it of thy **vine undressed**. For it is the jubile; it shall be **holy** unto you: ye shall eat the **increase** thereof out of the **field**. In the year of this jubile ye shall return every man unto his possession.

```
W H A U E S A E R C N I T S H
W N O O U H T E W O R G N T C
O O D Y T U N D R E S S E D I
L I S O T H D G F A M I L Y H
L S I T E R A Y C L T T I A W
A S R N O T E T E F H H B E D
H E T U H N H B I A E R U E Y
O S D E N A L F I Y R O J E A
U S R L D E B L R L E U S F G
T O E I E N I I A O O G I L R
O P A B O I A T T H F H H E A
F F P U J V F L H A S O T S P
T H E J U B I L E E N U U T E
H M I A L C O R P H R T B I S
E V E R Y M A N I N T L S E E
```

Secret Message

_____

_____

_____

_____

_____

_____

7

Brave Spies, Fearful Spies

Numbers 13:27–30

And **they** told him, and **said**, We came unto **the land** whither **thou sentest** us, and **surely it** floweth with milk and **honey**; and this is the **fruit of it**, Nevertheless the **people** be **strong** that dwell in the land, and the **cities** are **walled**, and very **great**: and **moreover** we saw the **children** of Anak there. The **Amalekites dwell in** the land of the **south**: and the **Hittites**, and the **Jebusites**, and the **Amorites**, dwell in the **mountains**: and the **Canaanites** dwell by the sea, and by the coast of **Jordan**. And **Caleb stilled** the people before **Moses**, and said, **Let us go** up at once, and **possess** it; for we are well able to **overcome** it.

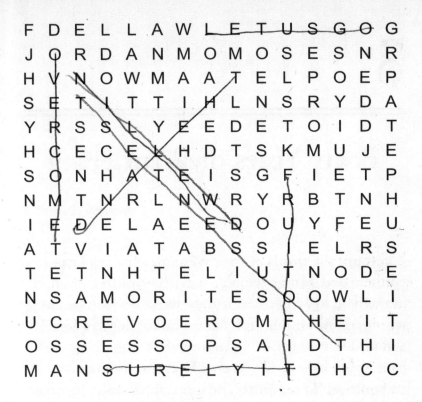

```
F D E L L A W L E T U S G O G
J O R D A N M O M O S E S N R
H V N O W M A A T E L P O E P
S E T I T T I H L N S R Y D A
Y R S S L Y E E D E T O I D T
H C E C E L H D T S K M U J E
S O N H A T E I S G F I E T P
N M T N R L N W R Y R B T N H
I E D E L A E E D O U Y F E U
A T V I A T A B S S I E L R S
T E T N H T E L I U T N O D E
N S A M O R I T E S O O W L I
U C R E V O E R O M F H E I T
O S S E S S O P S A I D T H I
M A N S U R E L Y I T D H C C
```

Secret Message

_____

_____

_____

_____

_____

_____

8

Forty Years of Wandering

Deuteronomy 29:1–4

These are the **words** of the **covenant**, which **the LORD commanded Moses to make** with the **children** of Israel in the **land of Moab**, beside the covenant which **he made** with **them in Horeb**. And Moses **called** unto **all Israel**, and **said** unto them, Ye **have seen** all that the LORD did before **your eyes in the land** of Egypt unto **Pharaoh**, and unto all his **servants**, and unto all his land; the **great temptations** which thine **eyes have** seen, the **signs**, and those great **miracles**: Yet the LORD hath **not given** you an **heart** to **perceive**, and **eyes to see**, and **ears to hear**, unto this day.

```
W H E A S E R V A N T S T D I
D N D G D T N A N E V O C T S
O N R E Y N H E M A D E O N T
M O O T L P A P W D V M G E G
I T H L L T L E I A I A R E
R G E E E A A D E K S R E D A
A I H M T A N C E H S A A L R
C V T I N A R D S T T O L I U
L E O N M E T T O W M N L H H
E N I M P L E H T F W O I C D
S H O R E B E S S E M O S I I
N C T E V A H S E Y E O R E A
S E Y E R U O Y Y V H E A D S
W T H E S E A R E I A L E B S
D E R N E P H A R A O H L S S
```

Secret Message

_____

_____

_____

_____

_____

_____

9

Hidden from Sight

Joshua 2:3–6

And the **king** of **Jericho** sent unto **Rahab**, **saying**, <u>**Bring forth**</u> the men that are come to thee, which are **entered** into **thine house**: for they **be come** to **search** out all the **country**. And the **woman took** the **two men**, and hid them, and **said thus**, **There** came **men unto** me, but I **wist not whence** they were: And it **came to pass** about the **time** of shutting of the **gate**, when it was **dark**, that the **men went out**: whither the men went **I wot not**: **pursue** after them **quickly**; for ye shall **overtake** them. But she had **brought** them up to the <u>**roof of the house**</u>, and <u>**hid them**</u> with the stalks of **flax**, which she had **laid** in **order** upon the **roof**.

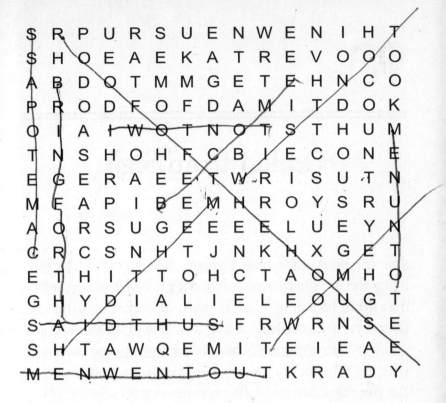

```
S R P U R S U E N W E N I H T
S H O E A E K A T R E V O O O
A B D O T M M G E T E H N C O
P R O D F O F D A M I T D O K
O I A I W O T N O T S T H U M
T N S H O H F C B I E C O N E
E G E R A E E T W R I S U T N
M F A P I B E M H R O Y S R U
A O R S U G E E E E L U E Y N
C R C S N H T J N K H X G E T
E T H I T T O H C T A Q M H O
G H Y D I A L I E L E Q U G T
S A I D T H U S F R W R N S E
S H T A W Q E M I T E I E A E
M E N W E N T O U T K R A D Y
```

Secret Message

_____

_____

_____

_____

_____

_____

10

One Great Shout

Joshua 6:20–23

The people shouted with a **great shout**, that the **wall fell** down **flat**, so that the **people went up** into the **city**, **every** man **straight** before him, and they **took** the city. And they **utterly destroyed** all that was in the city, **both man** and woman, **young and old**, and **ox, and sheep**, and ass, with the **edge** of the **sword**. But **Joshua** had said unto the **two men** that had **spied out** the **country**, Go into the **harlot's house**, and **bring out** thence the **woman**, and all that she hath, as ye sware unto her. And the **young men** that were **spies** went in, and **brought** out **Rahab**, and her **father**, and her **mother**, and her **brethren**, and **all that she had**.

N W Y O U N G A N D O L D E S
A H B K X L L E F L L A W V E
M C R O N A M O W A H T S E I
H I I O G N N P E T D S R P
T I N T N R D D H E U U R Y S
O M G U Y A A S P O H A T E
B R O U G H T B U H D P R B D
U Y U T L A E T S E E A L R G
A T T V H B N T S E I E O E E
G T T T O E O T F G P W R T A
R S L E W L R H H A S O U H U
E L W T R O H T E R T O L R H
A O A A Y L M Y A L H H T E S
T L H E Y T Y E O S I S E N O
F R D A E Y R T N U O C L R J

Secret Message

SCARLET THREAD

11

Celestial Standstill

Joshua 10:11–12, 14

And it **came to pass**, as they **fled** from before **Israel**, and were in the **going** down to **Bethhoron**, that the LORD **cast down** great **stones** from **heaven** upon them unto **Azekah**, and they **died**: they were more which died with **hailstones** than they whom the **children** of Israel **slew** with the **sword**. Then **spake Joshua** to the LORD **in the day** when the LORD **delivered** up the **Amorites** before the children of Israel, and he said in the **sight** of Israel, **Sun, stand** thou **still** upon **Gibeon**; and thou, **Moon**, in the **valley of Ajalon**. . . . And there was **no day** like that **before** it or **after** it, that the LORD **hearkened** unto the **voice** of a man: for the LORD **fought** for Israel.

```
W H I B C H I L D R E N C T G
S V H D E K A I W N N G H H O
T C A E O F D I E D F G J G I
O A E L R U O V L S I A L U N
N M D I L B A R S S E M L O G
E E E V E E D S E T T H E F C
S T N E H T Y W A M N O D A Y
E O E R P H J O S H U A N A I
T P K E G H N R F A G I A E I
I A R D A O N D N A T S N U S
R S A K R R E T F A J R D E P
O S E S N O E B I G T A E C A
M Z H O I N L L I T S E L I K
A S O C A S T D O W N L F O E
R M A E I N T H E D A Y L V N
```

Secret Message

_____

_____

_____

_____

_____

_____

12

Deadly Nap

Judges 4:17–18, 21

Howbeit Sisera **fled away** on his **feet** to the tent of **Jael** the wife of **Heber the Kenite**: for there was **peace between Jabin** the **king** of **Hazor** and the **house** of Heber the Kenite. And Jael went out to **meet Sisera**, and **said unto** him, Turn in, **my lord**, **turn in to me**; **fear not**. And when he had **turned** in unto her into the **tent**, she **covered** him with a **mantle**. . . . Then Jael Heber's **wife** took a **nail** of the tent, and **took** an **hammer** in her **hand**, and went **softly** unto him, and **smote** the nail into **his temples**, and **fastened** it into the **ground**: for he was **fast asleep** and **weary**. **So he died**.

```
W H I S T E M P L E S T E E F
E W D N F L E D A W A Y H E J
A I E P C H E L K P R O T F A
R T N S E P T I T I H I E A B
Y T R O M E R A P N N D E S I
E S U O H O L N R E A G E T N
T D T B S E T S K H A M M E R
I R D E I T L E A J O C H N E
E O A T S T H N T T A K E E C
B L K W E T D O N N S S O D I
W Y S E R E R I A S H A Z O R
O M F E A R N O T A R M F Y T
H I B N X R X O T N U D I A S
W E D N U O R G C O V E R E D
H Y L T F O S S O H E D I E D
```

Secret Message

Deborah

13

The Chosen Ones

Judges 7:4–5

And the LORD said unto **Gideon**, The **people** are yet <u>**too many**</u>; **bring** them down unto the **water**, and <u>**I will try them for thee**</u> there: and <u>**it shall be**</u>, that of <u>**whom I say**</u> unto thee, This shall <u>**go with thee**</u>, the same shall go <u>**with thee**</u>; and of **whomsoever** I say unto thee, This <u>**shall not go**</u> with thee, the same shall not go. So he <u>**brought down**</u> the people unto the water: and the LORD <u>**said unto**</u> Gideon, <u>**Every one**</u> that **lappeth** of the <u>**water with his**</u> **tongue**, as a <u>**dog lappeth**</u>, him **shalt** <u>**thou set**</u> by **himself**; **likewise** every one that **boweth** <u>**down upon**</u> his **knees** to **drink**.

```
L I K E W I S E T E S U O H T
H O N D O W N U P O N W T T M
A N I Y O I T F G K I D N H E
O O R N D L L W S N E M U E B
G B D R I L A P P E T H D R R
T G O W I T H T H E E E I E O
O L G W E R S T N S O N A L U
N E L R E Y H H A Y G P S E G
L U A P P T E F A G D U L V H
L G P P I H H S O L I T H E T
A N P W E E I W A R L D T R D
H O E H I M S E L F T B E Y O
S T T O O M A N Y E R H E O W
S I H H T I W R E T A W E N N
X X W H O M S O E V E R J E V
```

Secret Message

_____

_____

_____

_____

_____

_____

14

Ultimate Sacrifice

Judges 11:34–36

And **Jephthah** came to **Mizpeh** unto his house, and, **behold**, his daughter came out to <u>meet him</u> with **timbrels** and with **dances**: and she was his only **child**; beside her he had **neither** son nor daughter. And it <u>came to pass</u>, when <u>he saw her</u>, that he rent his **clothes**, and said, **Alas**, my daughter! thou hast **brought** me <u>very low</u>, and <u>thou art one</u> of them that **trouble** me: for I have **opened** my **mouth** unto the LORD, and I cannot <u>go back</u>. And she said unto him, My **father**, if thou hast opened thy mouth <u>unto the LORD</u>, do to me **according** to that which hath **proceeded** out of thy mouth; **forasmuch** as the LORD hath taken **vengeance** for <u>thee of thine</u> enemies.

```
C B W N E N I H T F O E E H T
L R E M E V E R Y L O W S J H
O O H H O I E O P E N E D E O
T U P E O U T N N D I I D P U
H G R E J L T H G M E P S H A
E H O L H A D H E E T S C T R
S T C B M H C N E R A U A H T
H L E U S E E C U P M N R A O
R R E O E N E D O S Z E C H N
E R D R H I S T A R H I D E E
A U E T B G E R H W D H M S T
E R D T O M O T A I H I A E L
R E H T A F I S O R M L N D X
D A N C E S E T K C A B O G X
U N T O T H E L O R D L I H C
```

Secret Message

_____

_____

_____

_____

_____

_____

15

A Wedding Banquet

Judges 14:10–14

So his **father** <u>went down</u> unto the **woman**: and **Samson** made **there** a **feast**. . . . They **brought** thirty **companions** to be with him. And Samson <u>**said unto them**</u>, I will now put forth a **riddle** unto you: if ye can **certainly declare** it me **within** the <u>**seven days**</u> of the feast, and <u>**find it out**</u>, then I will give you **thirty sheets** and thirty **change** of garments: But if ye cannot declare it me, then **shall** ye <u>**give me**</u> thirty sheets and thirty change of **garments**. And they <u>**said unto him**</u>, Put **forth** thy riddle, that <u>**we may**</u> <u>**hear it**</u>. And he said unto them, Out of the **eater** <u>**came**</u> <u>**forth**</u> **meat**, and out of the strong came forth **sweetness**. And they **could** not in <u>**three days**</u> **expound** the riddle.

```
M E A T W H T R O F E M A C S
H S W E E T N E S S E W C R A
T H I R T Y E R E H T I E A M
E T T W O R E H T A F T R T S
G X W E N T D O W N A H T H O
A S P C I N T G E E B I A S N
R N C O H N D I M D R N I E S
M O T O U A H N A M O W N L Y
E I E D U N N R Y I U D L D A
N N I D L L D G H S G A Y D D
T A E S Y A D E E R H T S I N
S P H T R O F E A S T E T R E
E M E V I G A E R A L C E D V
N O D F F I N D I T O U T T E
O C R X M I H O T N U D I A S
```

Secret Message

_____

_____

_____

_____

_____

_____

16

A Fool for Love

Judges 16:18–19

And when **Delilah** saw that he **had told** her **all his heart**, **she sent** and **called** for the **lords** of the **Philistines**, saying, **Come up** this once, for he **hath shewed** me all his heart. Then the lords of the **Philistines came** up **unto her**, and **brought money** in their **hand**. And she **made him** sleep **upon her knees**; and she **called for a man**, and she **caused** him to **shave** off the **seven locks** of his **head**; and she **began** to **afflict** him, and his **strength went from him**.

```
P W D E W E H S H T A H H O P
U H W E N T F R O M H I M N H
E A I A L S A Y I N G R A W I
M N A L S L T H E I E M S D L
O D E L I L A H R H A A E A I
C L S H L S K C O L N E V E S
M O H I I T T T E H J U N H T
I T E S D G N I T E W A A D I
H D S H Y U I G N T G V H E N
E A E E U N N S L E E P U S E
D H N A T E S O B U S A L U S
A O T R R S R O F D E L L A C
M T A T R D B R O U G H T C A
E E S N S T C I L F F A G T M
H U P O N H E R K N E E S H E
```

Secret Message

_____

_____

_____

_____

_____

_____

17

One Fell Swoop

Samson called unto the LORD, and said, O **Lord GOD**, **remember** me, I pray thee, and **strengthen** me, **I pray thee**, only **this once**, O God, that **I may be** at once **avenged** of the **Philistines** for my **two eyes**. And Samson **took hold** of the two **middle pillars** upon which the **house stood**, and on which it was **borne up**, of the one with his **right hand**, and of the **other** with his **left**. And Samson said, **Let me die** with the Philistines. And he **bowed himself** with all his **might**; and the **house fell** upon the **lords**, and upon all the **people** that were **therein**. So the **dead** which he **slew** at his **death** were more than they which he slew in **his life**.

```
H T W H A N T T H I S O N C E
L O R D G O D F L E S M I H S
P O U E C S I D N A H L A L A
C K T S O M H I S L I F E M V
S H H D E A T H M E I T M W E
R O E E N S T R E N G T H E N
A L R T I O T H E R I G H T G
L D E L D I T O D M S A M C E
L S I O E Y N B O W E D E A D
I H N T A T E L D D I M S L E
P S F R T R M I G H T E B L S
N E P G S E Y E O W T T P E D
L I M A Y B E H D C O O M D R
H O U S E F E L L I E E F R O
O M X B O R N E U P E X Z J L
```

Secret Message

_____

_____

_____

_____

_____

18

Ruth's Dedication

Ruth 1:16–19

And **Ruth** said, **Intreat** me not to **leave** thee, or to **return** from **following** after **thee**: for **whither** thou **goest**, I will go; and where thou **lodgest**, I will lodge: thy **people** shall be my people, and thy **God** my God: Where thou **diest**, will I die, and there will I be **buried**: the LORD do so to me, and **more** also, if **ought** but **death part** thee and me. When she saw that she was **stedfastly minded** to go with her, then she **left speaking** unto her. So they **two** went until **they came** to **Bethlehem**.

```
T F E L W H B E R E L E A V E
D I D N A O U M I A Y N D R U
L T H L I T R A P E L P O E P
V O E B E F I O R E T T H E S
Y T R R T S E I D A S T V E P
M L E D D T D O G H A H E T E
E T S E O G H E T R F E T O A
H A T H E O L U A S D E N T K
E E D D O D R F D J E U D H I
L R A E H E E X E X T G Y G N
H T K A H E T W D L S E D U G
T N S T I J U E N V R O L O G
E I I H E U R R I O B E T N L
B H U W E I N E M A C Y E H T
W M T W O N G N I W O L L O F
```

Secret Message

_____

_____

_____

_____

_____

_____

19

A Need Met

Ruth 2:15–19

And when she was <u>risen up</u> to glean, Boaz **commanded** his **young** men, **saying**, Let her glean even **among** the **sheaves**, and **reproach** her not: And let **fall** also some of the **handfuls** of **purpose** for her, and **leave** them, that she may **glean** them, and **rebuke** her not. <u>So she</u> gleaned in the **field** until even, and **beat** out that she had **gleaned**: and it was about an **ephah** of **barley**. And she **took** it up, and went into the **city**: and her <u>mother in law</u> saw what she had gleaned: and she **brought** forth, and gave to her that she had **reserved** after she was **sufficed**. And her mother in law said unto her, <u>Where hast</u> thou gleaned to day? and **where** <u>wroughtest thou</u>? **blessed** be he that did take **knowledge** of thee. And she <u>shewed her</u> mother in law <u>with whom</u> she had wrought, and said, The man's **name** with whom I wrought <u>to day</u> is **Boaz**.

```
T T O O K G L E A N E D W H A
S O T C N O R E H D E W E H S
A D S U F F I C E D U N E S L
H A O E T R E D L E I F G A U
E Y S Y V K N E P H A H D Y F
R D H I U A T D U U R U E I D
E T E B M H E M N H R O L N N
H R E M G I O H E G Y P W G A
W R O U G H T E S T T H O U H
I C O L W Y N L I A T E N S F
R R E H E Z L C R O W M K X E
B A T L W A L N I R E H T O M
N I R X F O V B L E S S E D A
W A T A E B D E V R E S E R N
B A M O N G R E P R O A C H E
```

Secret Message

_____

_____

_____

_____

_____

20

A Voice in the Night

1 Samuel 3:8–11

And the LORD called Samuel **again** the **third** time. And he **arose** and **went to Eli**, and said, **Here am I**; for thou **didst** call me. And Eli **perceived** that the LORD had called the **child**. **Therefore Eli said** unto Samuel, **Go, lie down**: and **it shall be**, if he **call thee**, that thou **shalt say**, Speak, LORD; for thy **servant** heareth. So Samuel went and lay down in his **place**. And the LORD **came**, and **stood**, and **called** as at **other times**, Samuel, **Samuel**. Then Samuel **answered, Speak**; for thy servant heareth. And the LORD said to Samuel, **Behold, I will do** a **thing** in **Israel**, at which both the **ears** of **every one** that **heareth** it shall **tingle**.

```
S E E H T L L A C B W H O W I
T E R S E E I S R A E L E T W
O H D U E H T E R A E H R E I
O I M P A R O S E I A R O E L
D A N T S O V H M F T D F L L
S H G I T S H A L L B E E D D
P C S A I S E L N M I R R I O
L R H P I R A T C T L E E A E
A O E I E N C S H I M W H S V
C L R H L A D A T A N S T I E
E A A D M D K Y C H E N D L R
G O L I E D O W N S I A G E Y
A M I L E O T T N E W N H U O
P E R C E I V E D E I T G L N
S E M I T D R I H T O S R A E
```

Secret Message

_____

_____

_____

_____

_____

_____

21

Prostrate before the Lord

1 Samuel 5:1–4

And the **Philistines took the ark** of God, and brought it from **Ebenezer** unto Ashdod. When the Philistines took the **ark of God**, they **brought** it into the **house** of **Dagon**, and set it by Dagon. And when they of **Ashdod arose early** on the **morrow**, behold, Dagon was **fallen upon his face** to the **earth** before the **ark of the LORD**. And they **took** Dagon, and set him in his **place again**. And when **they arose** early **on the morrow** morning, **behold**, Dagon was fallen upon his face to the **ground before the ark** of the LORD; and the **head of Dagon** and both the **palms** of his **hands** were **cut off** upon the **threshold**; only the stump of Dagon was left to him.

```
R T D A G A I N D O D H S A B
E O N W T H R L A A A D T H E
Z O U C A H O K G R R R W O F
E K O N T H E M O R R O W U O
N R R N S M C Y N F R L S S R
E A G E R O A I A R G M E E E
B E R L E R F D O R L O T N T
E H B L A N S M H A O E D I H
T T R A R I I A P C D S R T E
K K O F T N H H U O L D E S A
M O U E H G N T T O O N A I R
N O G A D F O D A E H A R L K
T T H H E F P L A C E H L I I
S R T A F E U L I T B E Y H S
X A R K O F T H E L O R D P X
```

Secret Message

_____

_____

_____

_____

_____

_____

22

A Giant Challenge

1 Samuel 17:43, 46, 49–51

And the **Philistine said** unto **David**, <u>**Am I a dog**</u>, that thou **comest** to me with **staves**? And the Philistine **cursed** David by <u>**his gods**</u>. . . . <u>**This day**</u> will the LORD **deliver** thee into <u>**mine hand**</u>; and I will **smite** thee. . . . David put <u>**his hand**</u> in <u>**his bag**</u>, and **took thence** a stone, and **slang** it, and smote the Philistine in his **forehead**, that the stone <u>**sunk into**</u> his forehead; and he <u>**fell upon his face**</u> to the **earth**. So David **prevailed** over the Philistine with a **sling** and with a **stone**, and **smote** the Philistine, and <u>**slew him**</u>; but there was no **sword** in the <u>**hand of David**</u>. . . . When the Philistines saw their **champion** was **dead**, <u>**they fled**</u>.

```
E C N E H T S U N K I N T O N
C O H D R O W S W H L D E O R
A M G A E W E H A S I O P T D
F E N H M V E A P V L U R A A
S S A C A P E N A I L S A D E
I T L T S A I D S L R M M N H
H I S B A G D O E A E O I M E
D L T L F A A F N S C T A I R
E D O E E D T D H M S E D N O
L N N D H W E A E I S P O E F
F A E H T S H V L T I L G H L
Y H I S R E V I L E D T I A I
E S N U A E H D M K O O T N S
H I C X E P R E V A I L E D G
T H I S D A Y X S D O G S I H
```

Secret Message

_____

_____

_____

_____

_____

_____

23

Can't Touch This

2 Samuel 6:5–9

And **David** and all the **house** of **Israel played** before the LORD on all **manner** of **instruments** made of fir **wood**, even on **harps**, and on **psalteries**, and on **timbrels**, and on **cornets**, and on **cymbals**. And when they came to **Nachon's threshingfloor, Uzzah** put forth his hand to the <u>ark of God</u>, and <u>took hold</u> of it; for the **oxen shook** it. And the **anger** of the LORD was **kindled** against Uzzah; and God **smote** him there for his **error**; and there he **died** by the ark of God. And David was **displeased**, **because** the LORD had made a **breach** upon Uzzah: and he **called** the **name** of the **place Perezuzzah** to <u>this day</u>. And David was **afraid** of the LORD that day.

```
A T W S H D O T O O K H O L D
N S H P C E I L H S E D R O L
G T H R M Y E S E I I O B X H
E I U A E A M I P A S S E E C
R M N H R S R B R L H D C N A
D B D S E E H F A A E A A H E
E R I E T L A I Z L L A U Y R
Y E V L D R S Z N P S D S D B
A L A T E N U D H G E E E E A
L S D N O Z Z M E R F L K F D
P O N H E R Z T E I D L H K R
R A C R D E A E M N D A O O O
M A E S U O H O I N T C T O R
N P D O G F O K R A H S S H R
S T E N R O C W X E T O M S E
```

Secret Message

_____

_____

_____

_____

_____

_____

24

Dancing in the Streets

2 Samuel 6:14–17

And **David danced** before the LORD with all his **might**; and David was **girded** with a **linen ephod**. So David and all the **house of Israel** brought up the **ark of the LORD** with shouting, and with the **sound** of the **trumpet**. And as the ark of the LORD **came** into the **city of David**, **Michal** Saul's **daughter looked through** a **window**, and saw **king** David **leaping** and **dancing** **before the LORD**; and she despised him in her **heart**. And they **brought** in the ark of the LORD, and set it in his **place**, in the **midst** of the **tabernacle** that David had **pitched** for it: and David **offered burnt offerings** and **peace** offerings **before** the LORD.

```
D W H D I V A D F O Y T I C C
L A H C I M E T R U M P E T A
A T U R E K D T H R O U G H M
S S U G O E R O F E B L N G E
E G T O H L O R D E D F I I C
L N L R O T L M P M I C P M A
C I H O U S E O F I S R A E L
A R N E H A H R E D T D E D P
N E L E P G T D N C I C L E S
R F B A N H F U A V A D H R D
E F B I G A O D A N C E D E E
B O K U T S K D T I C T P F D
A U O D R E R W O D N I W F R
T R A E H N A T S D I M N O I
B E F O R E T H E L O R D G G
```

Secret Message

_____

_____

_____

_____

_____

_____

25

Tempting Vision

2 Samuel 11:2–6

And it came to pass in an **eveningtide**, that **David arose** from **off his bed**, and **walked** <u>upon the roof</u> of the <u>king's house</u>: and from the **roof** he saw a woman **washing herself**; and the woman was very **beautiful** to **look** upon. And David sent and **enquired** after the woman. And <u>one said</u>, Is not this **Bathsheba**, the **daughter** of Eliam, the **wife** of **Uriah** the **Hittite**? And David sent **messengers**, and **took** her; and she came in unto him, and he <u>lay with her</u>; for she was **purified** from her **uncleanness**: and she **returned** unto her **house**. And the **woman conceived**, and sent and **told** David, and said, I am with **child**. And David sent to **Joab**, saying, Send me Uriah the Hittite.

U N C L E A N N E S S E F I W
P W H A T P U R I F I E D A R
O E L I A M D E N R U T E R D
N D N A M O W U D M Y I E L K
T E I L Y L F I R E E T O E A
H R D D U W V F S I H T D B E
E I E H R A I U H G A I E S S
R U V E D S O T U I T H O C U
O Q I R B H I A H G S R A H O
O N E S A I D H N H A B K I H
F E C E O N D I T U E O E L S
R I N L J G N A F O O R N D G
G A O F B E B W A L K E D A N
T T C L V L U F I T U A E B I
E S R E G N E S S E M T O O K

Secret Message

_____

_____

_____

_____

_____

_____

26

Solomon's Wise Request

1 Kings 3:11–14

Because thou hast asked this **thing**, and hast not **asked**
for thyself **long life**; neither hast asked **riches** for thyself,
nor hast asked the **life** of thine enemies; but hast asked
for thyself understanding to **discern judgment**; **behold**, I
have done **according** to thy **words**: lo, I have **given** thee a
wise and an understanding **heart**; so that there was none
like thee before thee, **neither** after thee shall any **arise**
like unto thee. And I have also given thee that which
thou hast not asked, both riches, and **honour**: so that
there shall not be any among the **kings** like unto thee **all
thy days**. And if thou **wilt walk** in my **ways**, to **keep** my
statutes and my **commandments**. . .then I will **lengthen**
thy days.

```
W C H I C H Q S E T U T A T S
D O L O N G L I F E D U E Y Y
I M E N W T T R A V L E A L A
S M E D I T H O J E O W R R D
C A K U S S I A L T H S I E Y
E N M I E T N O N S E E S E H
R D E S N O G E L H B O E M T
N M O H N G M S C W I S D O L
K E E P T G S I M W O R D S L
F N I R D G R U O N O H S G A
D T T U H A N N D T X X F I A
E S J P L N T E R L O N L V Y
K O W I L T W A L K H E A E A
S L F O M N E I T H E R S N D
A E E E R H A C C O R D I N G
```

Secret Message

_____

_____

_____

_____

_____

_____

27

The House of the Lord

1 Kings 7:48–51

And **Solomon** made all the **vessels** that pertained unto the **house** of the Lord: the **altar** of gold, and the **table** of **gold**, whereupon the **shewbread** was, and the **candlesticks** of **pure** gold, **five** on the **right** side, and five on the **left**, before the **oracle**, with the **flowers**, and the **lamps**, and the **tongs** of gold, and the **bowls**, and the **snuffers**, and the **basons**, and the **spoons**, and the **censers** of pure gold; and the **hinges** of gold, both for the **doors** of the **inner** house, the most **holy** place, and for the doors of the house, to **wit**, of the **temple**. So was **ended** all the **work** that **king** Solomon **made** for the house of the Lord.

H	O	W	C	E	N	S	E	R	S	E	G	N	I	H
D	M	A	N	Y	Y	F	E	A	R	S	T	O	T	A
L	O	H	D	I	S	I	E	D	I	T	S	T	G	A
R	K	O	E	S	H	V	L	O	L	K	O	O	S	O
I	M	L	R	O	E	E	B	N	C	T	L	P	O	S
G	B	Y	U	S	W	I	A	I	L	D	O	D	L	T
H	H	I	S	S	B	O	T	W	K	O	M	W	N	F
T	P	E	E	R	R	S	S	I	N	H	O	U	S	E
O	L	N	A	E	E	L	N	S	H	B	N	P	E	L
S	R	A	T	L	A	G	O	U	M	E	I	U	L	A
L	O	R	D	C	D	X	S	X	F	I	N	R	P	M
R	I	N	M	A	P	G	W	I	T	F	N	E	M	P
I	A	A	F	R	N	E	N	D	E	D	E	R	E	S
C	D	F	L	O	W	E	R	S	N	E	R	R	T	O
E	S	L	T	W	O	R	K	B	A	S	O	N	S	W

Secret Message

_____

_____

_____

_____

_____

_____

28

Solomon and Sheba

1 Kings 10:4–8

And when the **queen** of **Sheba** had seen all **Solomon's** wisdom, and the house that he had **built,** and the meat of his **table,** and the **sitting** of his **servants,** and the **attendance** of his **ministers,** and their **apparel,** and his **cupbearers,** and his **ascent** by which he went up unto the **house of the LORD**; there was no more **spirit** in her. And she said to the king, It was a **true report** that I heard in mine **own land** of thy acts and of thy wisdom. **Howbeit** I **believed** not the **words,** until I came, and **mine eyes** had seen it: and, behold, **the half was not told me**: thy wisdom and **prosperity exceedeth** the fame which I heard. **Happy** are thy men, happy are these thy servants, which **stand continually** before thee, and **that hear thy wisdom.**

```
H O W M O D S I W Y H T D I D
H A P P A R E L D N A T S T H
A E Q S N O M O L O S U R E T
P B C E T L E X C E E D E T H
P B E O O E F L A H E H T P A
Y U E H N H C N B C O R S R T
Q I D F S T S N U A O H I O H
M L E E A F I P A P T T N S E
I T V S W O B N E D I B I P A
N A E P A E W R U E N T M E R
E T I I A S E N B A T E M R E
E S L R T U C W L I L D T I S
Y O E I R O O E N A L L L T O
E R B T M H O G N O N N Y Y A
S E R V A N T S T T S D R O W
```

Secret Message

_____

_____

_____

_____

_____

_____

29

Voice of God

1 Kings 19:10–12

And he said, I have been very **jealous** for the <u>LORD God</u> of **hosts**: for the **children** of **Israel** have **forsaken** thy **covenant, thrown** down **thine altars**, and **slain** thy **prophets** with the sword; and I, <u>**even I only**</u>, <u>**am left**</u>; and they **seek** <u>**my life**</u>, to take <u>**it away**</u>. And he said, Go **forth**, and **stand** upon the mount before the LORD. And, behold, the LORD **passed** by, and a **great** and **strong** <u>**wind rent**</u> the **mountains**, and **brake** in pieces the **rocks** before the LORD; but the LORD was <u>**not in the wind**</u>: and after the wind an **earthquake**; but the LORD was not in the earthquake: And after the earthquake <u>**a fire**</u>; but the LORD was not <u>**in the fire**</u>: and after the fire a <u>**still small voice**</u>.

```
W N O T I N T H E W I N D H E
G T N A N E V O C L R E O E Y
R O C K S M Y L I F E K G P A
E E E S T E H P O R P A D A W
A W V N W S A S V E L R R S A
T L I E I J N A L H E B O S T
H I T K N H I I L K D I L E I
N N G A D I T W A H S C E D N
T T H S R E O U M T H W O R J
D H E R E S Q N S I N O F E N
T E R O N H H O L F S U A W S
K F I F T E H D L Y O L O T L
O I F R R D R C I A O R A M M
E R A M L E F T T U H N T I T
O E H G N O R T S T D I M H N
```

Secret Message

_____

_____

_____

_____

_____

_____

30

The Captain and the Slave Girl

2 Kings 5:1–4

Now Naaman, **captain** of the **host** of the **king** of Syria, was a **great** man with his **master**, and **honourable, because** by him the LORD had **given deliverance** unto Syria: he was also a **mighty** man in **valour**, but he was a **leper**. And the **Syrians** had gone out by **companies**, and had **brought away captive** out of the **land** of Israel a **little maid**; and she **waited** on **Naaman's wife**. And she said unto her **mistress, Would** God my lord **were** with the **prophet** that is in **Samaria**! for he would **recover** him of his **leprosy**. And **one went** in, and told his lord, **saying, Thus and** thus said the maid that is of the land **of Israel**.

```
D W H Y O P S E M E S S E N G
L E M E S R E P E L R H T O L
U V L I D O T H G U O R B N A
O I C I G P R A S N A I R Y S
W T O R V H M P O V A L O U R
R P M D E E T U E I E A O A N
E A P I I T R Y R L S N D R A
C C A T S A S A E O U D N W D
O G N W B T M A N A A M A N S
V N I L A A R E M C C Y S S H
E I E I S S G E L N E N U T H
R Y S W I R H O S T B E H W K
E A J F E R E W O S T V T I R
D S O A A N C A P T A I N F N
R I T V D E T I A W E G L E R
```

Secret Message

_____

_____

_____

_____

_____

_____

31

A Leper Healed

2 Kings 5:13–15

And his **servants** came **near**, and **spake** unto him, and said, My **father**, if the **prophet** had **bid** thee do some **great thing**, wouldest thou not have done it? how much **rather** then, when he **saith** to thee, **Wash**, and be **clean**? Then went he **down**, and **dipped** himself <u>seven times</u> in **Jordan**, according to the **saying** of the <u>man of God</u>: and his **flesh** came **again** like unto the flesh of a **little child**, and he was clean. And he **returned** to the man of God, he and all his **company**, and **came**, and **stood before** him: and he said, **Behold**, now I **know** that there is no God in all the **earth**, but in **Israel**: now therefore, I **pray** thee, take a **blessing** of thy servant.

```
N L I T T L E R E H T A R B R
S E V E N T I M E S W H A E T
Y N A P M O C W A S T H T F E
T A E R G B E H O L D U D O L
E G N I Y A S N A D R O J R P
E A R N S T O O D N G A A A E M
A I E K A P S N E F H T R A E
D N P S I P T D O C A M E O S
E I R T T I N N O N U K N O W
P N A D H E A R T H T E W K I
P N Y G O M V F T E H P O R P
I S Y L E A R S I R I I D A H
D L I H C L E A N X N X O A S
I D E B L E S S I N G L J F A
B E L F H S E L F A T H E R W
```

Secret Message

_____

_____

_____

_____

_____

_____

32

The Missing Enemy

2 Kings 7:5–7

And they **rose up** in the **twilight,** to go unto the camp of the **Syrians**: and **when** they were **come** to the **uttermost part** of the **camp of Syria, behold,** there was **no man there**. For the LORD had **made** the host of the Syrians to **hear** a **noise** of **chariots,** and a noise of **horses, even** the noise of a **great host**: and they said one to **another,** Lo, the **king of Israel** hath **hired against** us the **kings** of the **Hittites,** and the kings of the **Egyptians,** to come upon us. **Wherefore they arose and fled** in the twilight, and **left their tents,** and their horses, and their asses, even the camp as it was, and **fled for their life**.

```
W H K I N G S O R O F D E L F
K T F I L O R D R S C T E E P
D I R T S N I A G A R F V U I
S S N A I R Y S M A T E E T C
O D S G P H V P E T N S S H E
R L E E O D O H H A O O N E T
W O T R T F H E N R M R A I A
T H S S S I I O T R A A I R H
E E E Y O R T S E S N Y T L A
S B R N T H D T R Y T E P I N
E I R E E E T M I A H H Y F D
A M N R R U I A A H E T G E F
S T O I R A H C E D R L E A L
S N H C S H W H E R E F O R E
A D F L E T W I L I G H T D D
```

Secret Message

_____

_____

_____

_____

_____

_____

33

Getting Ready to Build

1 Chronicles 22:14–16

Now, behold, in my **trouble <u>I have</u>** prepared <u>**for the house**</u> of the LORD an **hundred thousand talents <u>of gold</u>**, and a thousand thousand talents <u>**of silver**</u>; and of **brass <u>and iron</u>** without **weight**; for it is in **abundance**: timber also and stone have I prepared; and thou mayest add thereto. **Moreover <u>there are</u> workmen** with thee in abundance, **hewers** and **workers <u>of stone</u> <u>and timber</u>**, and all <u>**manner of**</u> **cunning <u>men for</u> every** manner of work. Of the gold, the silver, and the brass, and the iron, there <u>**is no**</u> **number. Arise therefore, <u>and be</u>** **doing**, and the LORD <u>**be with thee**</u>.

```
E B D N A W H P Y F G N I O D
S S A R B W M O R E O V E R R
U E R A E R E H T E N R O A O
O T R O U B L E S O P L T D F
H S A B V I M D R N D A O H N
T A R L E L R I O W E B R C E
E D E E T W D E T O R U U E M
E B V U K N I H B D D N I V D
O S L T A R E T N M N D W A L
F L I I A R O A H I U A O H O
S D S R E L S W N T H N R I G
T N F F A U E G A H H C K O F
O U O F O R E N N A M E M S O
N R T H G I E W T E E V E R Y
E F T O H E W E R S R G N O D
```

Secret Message

_____

_____

_____

_____

_____

_____

34

Promise of Healing

2 Chronicles 7:14–16

If **my people**, **which** are **called** by **my name**, **shall humble themselves**, **and pray**, **and seek** **my face**, and **turn from** their **wicked ways**; **then** **will I hear** from **heaven**, and will **forgive** **their sin**, and **will heal** **their land**. Now **mine eyes** shall be **open**, and mine **ears attent unto** the **prayer** that is **made** in this **place**. For now have I **chosen** and **sanctified** this **house**, that my name may be there for ever: and mine eyes and mine **heart** shall **be there** **perpetually**.

P R A Y E R W H O B D N E H T
U E I F O R G I V E H L L O T
Y A R P D N A T I U H L P E T
H P O P O U S F M C L E O H E
T H L T E A I B T A N S E Y E
G M N A H T L O H L E M P W N
E U Y I C E U S W L S A Y I E
A D K N S E I A I E O D M C V
R T A E A R H R L D H E A K A
S S T R E M I V L L C F A E E
E D C E W S E E I A Y S H D H
S O S H N S D E H M N E Y N T
U O I T S T A N E T N D N A C
O C H E A R T L A E H L L I W
H T I B F Y T U R N F R O M M

Secret Message

_____

_____

_____

_____

_____

_____

35

Hand of God

Ezra 8:21–23

Then I **proclaimed** a fast there, at the **river** of **Ahava**, that we might **afflict ourselves before** our God, to seek of him a **right** way for us, and for our <u>little ones</u>, and for all our **substance**. For I was **ashamed** to **require** of the <u>king a band</u> of **soldiers** and **horsemen** to help us against the **enemy** in the way: **because** we had **spoken** unto the king, **saying**, <u>The hand of our God is upon all them for good that seek him</u>; but his **power** and his **wrath** is against all them that **forsake** him. So we **fasted** and **besought** our God for this: and he was **intreated** of us.

```
L K W D O G R U O F O H E A D
M I H K E E S T A H T R E F E
W N T N E M E S R O H H S F T
A G N T E S I E D Z R P G L A
A A O G L N R A O N O I O I E
B B P N G E E F L K A U W C R
E A U H Q S O M E C R H N T T
F N S U U R E N Y S O A E T N
O D I A S H A M E D T R E H I
R R C A T V W L N S H E P G T
E E K L A R V A B S K E D U F
B E L H A E O U F O R G O O D
R A A T S V S O L D I E R S A
S A H G N I Y A S F A S T E D
F E J O U R E W O P R N E B Y
```

Secret Message

_____

_____

_____

_____

_____

_____

36

City in Ruins

Nehemiah 2:2–5

Wherefore the **king said** unto me, Why is thy **countenance** sad, seeing thou **art not sick**? this is **nothing** else but **sorrow of** heart. Then I was very sore **afraid**, and said unto the king, Let the **king live** for ever: why should not my countenance **be sad**, when **the city**, the place of my **fathers' sepulchres**, lieth **waste**, and the **gates thereof** are **consumed with fire**? Then the king said unto me, For what dost thou make **request**? So I **prayed** to the **God of heaven**. And I said unto the king, If it **please** the king, and if thy **servant** have **found favour** in **thy sight**, that thou **wouldest** send me unto **Judah**, unto the **city of my** fathers' sepulchres, that I **may build it**.

```
E T S A W W W I T H F I R E A
N S H H F A S O R R O W O F F
T E P T E A O S T S E U Q E R
T D V C H A T D I A R D N E A
H L E A O G R H R M E I A H I
D U M H E U I T E N H A Y S D
I O A F V H N S O R T S M E E
A W Y W A O F T Y B S E F P I
S T B D T V H O E H E R O U H
G K U S F I O S D N T V Y L I
N J I N N O A U G O A A T C A
I C L G R D U T R A G N I H X
K E D E M U S N O C R T C R X
E V I L G N I K D P R A Y E D
E S T H E C I T Y P L E A S E
```

Secret Message

_____

_____

_____

_____

_____

_____

37

Courageous Queen

Esther 4:14–16

For if thou **altogether holdest** thy **peace** at **this time**, then **shall** there **enlargement** and **deliverance arise** to the Jews from **another place**; but thou and thy **father's house** shall be **destroyed**: and who **knoweth whether** thou art come to the **kingdom** for such a time as this? Then **Esther** bade them **return Mordecai** this **answer**, Go, **gather** together all the Jews that are **present** in **Shushan**, and **fast ye for** me, and **neither eat nor drink three days, night** or day: I also and my **maidens** will fast **likewise**; and so will I go in unto the king, which is not **according** to the law: and if I perish, **I perish**.

```
A D K N O W E T H H O W W A
D N E N R E S U O H S E H S H
E T S L I U E H F A T H E R S
S P I W I R T R U H E A T E I
T R W R E V D E H S L E H H R
R E E R E R E R R T H C E T E
O S K G N I D R O C C A R O P
Y E I L A T E G A N D E N N I
E N L A R G E M E N T P G A T
D T H I S T I M E T C A C S H
A O R E H T I E N M T E E H G
R O F E Y T S A F H D D C A I
I O R E H T S E E R L A A L N
S N E D I A M R O O R Y L L D
E K I N G D O M H E C S P A I
```

Secret Message

_____

_____

_____

_____

_____

_____

38

Esther Approaches the King

Esther 7:1–4

So the **king** and **Haman** came to **banquet** with **Esther** the **queen**. And the king said again unto Esther on the **second day** at the banquet of **wine**, What is thy **petition**, queen Esther? and it shall be **granted** thee: and what is thy **request**? and it shall be **performed**, even to the **half** of the **kingdom**. Then Esther the queen **answered** and said, If I have found **favour** in thy **sight**, O king, and if it **please** the king, let my **life** be **given** me at my petition, and my **people** at my request: For we are **sold**, I and my people, to be **destroyed**, to be **slain**, and to **perish**. But if we had been sold for **bondmen** and **bondwomen**, I had held my **tongue**, although the **enemy** could not countervail the king's **damage**.

```
W H A A N S W E R E D T P N P
P E T I T I O N E R S E O E E
T E U Q N A B E F I L S N E R
A B O N D W O M E N L A P U F
D N O C E S O Y S I S E D Q O
E A S F S V I O G A N L E R R
D M L I D K I I N L O P T E M
N A G A H A S G I S U E N Q E
H H M O D G N I K R U S A U D
S G R E H T S E P I V E R E T
I E D E Y O R T S E D U G S T
R O N B O N D M E N O M O T H
E R D I E G C A I V Y P X X G
P H A M W U L I A S A C L A I
D A M A G E A F O T D R D E S
```

Secret Message

_____

_____

_____

_____

_____

_____

39

Job Is Blessed

Job 42:12–16

So the Lord **blessed** the **latter end** of **Job** more than his **beginning**: for he had **fourteen** thousand **sheep**, and **six** thousand **camels**, and a **thousand yoke** of **oxen**, and a thousand she **asses**. He had also **seven sons** and **three daughters**. And he **called** the **name** of the first, **Jemima**; and the name of the second, **Kezia**; and the name of the third, Kerenhappuch. And in **all** the **land** were no **women found** so **fair** as the daughters of Job: and their **father** gave them inheritance among their brethren. After this lived Job an hundred and **forty years**, and **saw** his sons, and his sons' sons, even **four** generations.

```
J E M I M A W H A T D S I D F
Y S A T S A W A N C L L A D O
S E S S A I M O W E O D U A R
D L A D I J O B M B E N J U T
E O B R S X N A R E E U S G Y
L P D O S E C N S E N O I H F
L T N H V E L O R I A F R T D
A T A E E R H T O O K O X E N
C E S V D E R F D L Y U T R P
H I U R N N O E E A A R G S E
Y F O R E U M O S I M T H I E
O L H M R A X X S Z A E T J H
K J T S N O S A E E L E S E S
E L O A C D N A L K L N K A R
G N I N N I G E B F A T H E R
```

Secret Message

_____

_____

_____

_____

_____

_____

40

Rooted in Righteousness

Psalm 1:1–5

Blessed is the man that **walketh** not in the **counsel** of the **ungodly**, nor **standeth** in the way of **sinners**, nor **sitteth** in the **seat** of the **scornful**. But his **delight** is in the law of the LORD; and in his law doth he **meditate** day and **night**. And he **shall** be like a **tree planted** by the **rivers** of **water**, that **bringeth forth** his **fruit** in his **season**; his **leaf** also shall not **wither**; and **whatsoever** he doeth shall **prosper**. The ungodly are not so: but are like the **chaff** which the **wind driveth away**. **Therefore** the ungodly shall not stand in the **judgment**, nor sinners in the **congregation** of the **righteous**.

```
S C W B R I N G E T H H A T D
C O N G R E G A T I O N H O E
O U I C W S V H P L A N T E D
R N G H H I E E W I T H E R T
N S H A T R N S O H L I K S P
F E T F E E I D E S S E L B S
U L N F V T T G A A T A A L M
L S O A I A R T H Y T A W F S
S R S H R T E T I T A P H A L
E R A L D I E H A S E R L W Y
T N E M G D U J U N G O D L Y
I P S N N E R I V E R S U P E
U N T A N M O T H D E P U S N
R G T H G I L E D O R E T A W
F S L L A H S D L H T R O F Y
```

Secret Message

_____

_____

_____

_____

_____

_____

41

Despair

Psalm 22:1–6

My God, my God, why hast thou **forsaken me**? why art **thou so** far from **helping me**, and from the **words** of my **roaring**? O my God, **I cry in** the day **time**, but thou **hearest** not; and in the **night season**, and **am not** silent. But thou **art holy**, O thou that **inhabitest** the **praises** of **Israel**. Our **fathers trusted in thee**: they trusted, and **thou didst** deliver them. They **cried unto thee**, and were **delivered**: they trusted in thee, and **were not** confounded. But **I am a worm**, and no man; a **reproach** of men, and **despised** of the **people**.

```
W F A T H E R S H O I N T H E
T H O U D I D S T N E T W S T
E D E R E V I L E D H S I I S
R T E A S S E A S O N L N N D
O M M I Y A E N U T E T I T R
A U G R R L K S S N C D Y H O
R S N A O C O E T O N E R E W
I E I T I W T H N D T T C E H
N E P O O I A F T M H S I P E
G N L R B T O M Y R E U I P L
T N E A O U H G A S A R G E W
H I H N N A O E I I R T A O O
G N M D R D C A E D E R S P O
I A E E F T R H H I S S P L S
N D E S I P S E D I T A L E M
```

Secret Message

_____

_____

_____

_____

_____

_____

42

Praise the Lord!

Psalm 95:3–9

For the LORD is a **great God**, and a **great King** **above all** gods. In his **hand are** the deep **places** of the **earth**: the **strength** of the **hills** is his also. The **sea is his**, and **he made it**: and his **hands formed** the **dry land**. O **come**, let us **worship** and **bow down**: let us **kneel** before the LORD our **maker**. For **he is our God**; and we are the **people** of his **pasture**, and the **sheep** of his hand. To day if ye will hear his **voice**, **harden** not your **heart**, as in the **provocation**, and as in the day of **temptation** in the **wilderness**: When your **fathers tempted** me, **proved** me, and **saw my work**.

```
T H D R Y L A N D G A I N S E
P S P I H S R O W R B A W M L
M S D N A H D I G E O S O A A
S H E E P Y E T N A V C D K P
S N E C P T V A I T E O W E M
A S O I A K O C K G A I O R N
E I W I S L R O T O L P B K E
H H A T T O P V A D L K R I D
F S K N U A U O E E E O D E R
A I O N R H T R R R W M T C A
T A F N E O N P G Y A P R I H
H E M A D E I T M O M D I O S
E S R E S T L W O E D T N V F
R T H S E E A R T H T L O A R
S L L I H S T R E N G T H D H
```

Secret Message

_____

_____

_____

_____

_____

_____

43

Prosperous Woman

Proverbs 31:11–17

The **heart** of her **husband** doth **safely trust <u>in her</u>**, so that he **shall have <u>no need</u>** of **spoil**. She will do <u>**him good**</u> and <u>**not evil**</u> all the days of her life. She **seeketh wool**, and **flax**, and **worketh willingly** with her **hands**. She is like the **merchants' ships**; she **bringeth** her food from afar. She **riseth** also while it is yet **night**, and **giveth** meat to her **household**, and a **portion** to her **maidens**. She **considereth** a **field**, and **buyeth** it: with the **fruit** of her hands she **planteth** a **vineyard**. She **girdeth** her **loins** with strength, and **strengtheneth** her arms.

```
T N I G H T D N A B S U H H S
F E P M T T R L I V E T O N S
F L S E E K E T H I E N I D W
R I A C Y R F R I N O O N I O
U O F X U H C I E N L A L H O
I P E H B T T H E D H L E T L
T S L O O E T E A L I E F E A
S R Y U V G D I D N D S R K R
T P A S N N U M G R T O N R D
H O I E U I S L A R I S W O O
T R R H H R Y Y U I M G O W C
E T A O S B E S N I D G S F A
S I P L A N T E T H M E V A H
I O R D I H T E V I G A N B O
R N V V E W H S H A L L A S T
```

Secret Message

_____

_____

_____

_____

_____

_____

44

Poor but Wise

Ecclesiastes 9:13–18

This **wisdom** have I <u>**seen also**</u> <u>**under the sun**</u>, and it **seemed** great unto me: There was a <u>**little city**</u>, and <u>**few men**</u> within it; and there came a <u>**great king**</u> **against** it, and **besieged** it, and built great **bulwarks** against it: Now there was **found** in it a <u>**poor wise**</u> man, and he by his wisdom **delivered** the city; yet no man **remembered** that same poor man. Then said I, Wisdom is **better** than **strength**: **nevertheless** the poor man's wisdom is **despised**, and his **words** are <u>**not heard**</u>. The words of <u>**wise men**</u> are heard in <u>**quiet more**</u> than the <u>**cry of him**</u> that **ruleth** among **fools**. Wisdom is better than **weapons** of war: but one **sinner destroyeth** much **good**.

```
W H A P O O R W I S E H T T I
Q U I E T M O R E T T R N D R
Y G N I K T A E R G L U E E E
A T O D E D M E N S C L M S T
G C I O E E N E R R I E W T T
A N D C D R R O Y B M T E R E
I W E E E T T O T B S H F O B
N I R M S L F H E H T H E Y D
S S E L E H T R E V E N W E E
T D V R I S E T S S I A G T S
T O I M E D I R I O U E R H I
F M L S D R O W N L I N T D P
S E E N A L S O N S L O O F S
H I D S N O P A E W S B O O E
S K R A W L U B R K F O U N D
```

Secret Message

_____

_____

_____

_____

_____

_____

45

Sheltered by Love

Song of Songs 2:3–7

As the **apple tree** among the **trees** of the **wood,** so is my **beloved** among the sons. I **sat down** under his **shadow** with **great delight,** and **his fruit** was **sweet** to **my taste.** **He brought** me to the **banqueting house, and his** banner **over me** **was love.** Stay me with **flagons, comfort** me with **apples:** for I am **sick of love.** His **left hand** is under **my head,** and his **right hand** doth **embrace** me. I **charge** you, O ye **daughters** of **Jerusalem,** by the **roes,** and by the **hinds** of the **field,** that ye **stir** not up, nor **awake** my love, till he **please.**

```
J  S  A  T  D  O  W  N  W  S  T  I  R  S  H
E  E  G  I  E  S  A  E  L  P  D  T  I  A  T
R  E  R  U  M  W  O  O  D  A  R  C  G  E  R
U  R  E  R  B  E  O  S  E  O  K  S  H  M  E
S  T  A  F  R  E  I  H  F  O  R  E  T  R  S
A  E  T  S  A  T  Y  M  F  E  M  L  H  E  E
L  P  T  I  C  M  O  L  T  N  E  P  A  V  W
E  T  P  H  E  C  O  H  S  I  S  P  N  O  O
M  N  E  L  G  V  G  B  D  N  U  A  D  T  C
G  N  I  T  E  U  Q  N  A  B  O  A  I  H  D
N  H  T  H  A  T  O  E  I  N  H  G  A  G  L
S  I  H  D  N  A  R  R  K  S  N  R  A  I  E
S  N  D  E  V  O  L  E  B  A  G  E  O  L  I
C  D  W  A  S  L  O  V  E  E  W  H  R  E  F
A  S  P  T  E  R  L  E  F  T  H  A  N  D  S
```

Secret Message

_____

_____

_____

_____

_____

_____

46

Advance Man

Isaiah 40:1–5

Comfort ye, comfort ye my **people**, saith **your** God. **Speak** ye **comfortably** to **Jerusalem**, and cry unto her, that her **warfare** is **accomplished**, that her **iniquity** is **pardoned**: for she hath **received** of the LORD's **hand double** for all her sins. The **voice** of him that **crieth** in the **wilderness, Prepare** ye the way of the LORD, make **straight** in the **desert** a **highway** for our God. **Every valley shall** be **exalted**, and every **mountain** and hill shall be made low: and the **crooked** shall be made straight, and the **rough places** plain: And the **glory** of the LORD shall be **revealed**, and all **flesh** shall see it **together**: for the **mouth** of the LORD hath **spoken** it.

```
F W H H O S V I N T R O U G H
H L A E N H M O U T H N H D T
Y N E W Y A E W I T E I I E E
D E H S I L P M O C C A G S I
S T L A H L B T O G E T H E R
E X A L T E D A M Y J N W R C
P R E P A R E E T E E U A T E
S P E A K V C I R R U O Y R D
E Y N R T R U U F N O M A U E
L L R D O Q S P F I E F L P V
B L E O I A D I L Y R S M E I
U S K N L T H G I A R T S O E
O E I E A G I A W H C E S P C
D P M D E L A E V E R E V L E
R O P H E C Y N E K O P S E R
```

Secret Message

_____

_____

_____

_____

_____

_____

47

Trust God

Blessed is the man that **trusteth** in the LORD, and **whose hope** the LORD is. For <u>he shall</u> be as a <u>tree planted</u> by the **waters**, and that **spreadeth** out <u>her roots</u> by the **river**, and <u>shall not</u> see <u>when heat</u> **cometh**, but <u>her leaf</u> shall be **green**; and shall not be **careful** in the **year** of **drought**, **neither** shall **cease from yielding fruit**. The **heart** is **deceitful** above all **things**, and **desperately wicked**: who can know it? I the LORD **search** the heart, I try the **reins**, even to give **every** man **according** <u>to his ways</u>, and according to the fruit of his **doings**.

```
T W R H E A R T M H Y R E V E
H O P E C D A T O N L L A H S
I R E V I R R F R E T H T P O
N C D Y D N A O F E K T R I H
G N E G L E S E L R C E E O W
S A S A L U S U S G A T E N Q
R R S R S U F P E D G S P H T
W H E N H E A T E N D U L E O
R H L T R E I T I R N R A S H
C D B A A U H D O E A T N H I
D O C J R W R U I U C T T A S
D I M F A O G T H I N E E L W
T N H E C H H W I C K E D L A
I G S C T E B G N I D L E I Y
O S A O R H K H E R R O O T S
```

Secret Message

_____

_____

_____

_____

_____

_____

48

Time of Despair

Lamentations 5:1–8

Remember, O L<small>ORD</small>, what is come upon us: **consider**, and behold our **reproach**. Our **inheritance** is **turned** to **strangers**, our **houses** to **aliens**. We are **orphans** and **fatherless**, our **mothers** are as widows. We have **drunken** our **water** for **money**; our **wood** is sold unto us. Our **necks** are under **persecution**: we **labour**, and have no rest. We have **given** the hand to the **Egyptians**, and to the **Assyrians**, to be **satisfied** with **bread**. Our **fathers** have **sinned**, and are not; and we have **borne** their **iniquities**. **Servants** have **ruled** over us: there is none that doth **deliver** us out of their hand.

```
T D E N N I S H E F A S R D E
S E R V A N T S A H N M O D G
Y L E O F W H T O A M O N E Y
A I P T P S H U H C W O U L P
N V R T R E S P Y D E N R U T
S E O B R E R E B M E M E R I
N R A S S O E S L R O U S N A
A G C H T G H O E R D R I S N
I N H E R I T A N C E Q J U S
R E D I S N O C L G U H D G M
Y K E W D N M A N I I T T T O
S N N A J E B A T R E V I A U
S U E T S O R I B O R N E O F
A R A E U T E L N E C K S N N
B D E R S S A T I S F I E D M
```

Secret Message

_____

_____

_____

_____

_____

_____

49

Precious and Perfect

Ezekiel 28:13–15

Thou hast been in **Eden** the **garden** of God; **every precious** stone was thy **covering**, the **sardius**, **topaz**, and the **diamond**, the **beryl**, the **onyx**, and the **jasper**, the **sapphire**, the **emerald**, and the **carbuncle**, and **gold**: the **workmanship** of thy **tabrets** and of thy **pipes** was **prepared** in thee in the day that thou wast **created**. Thou art the **anointed cherub** that **covereth**; and I have set thee so: thou wast upon the **holy mountain** of God; thou hast **walked** up and **down** in the **midst** of the **stones** of **fire**. Thou wast **perfect** in thy **ways** from the day that thou wast created, <u>**till iniquity**</u> was **found** <u>**in thee**</u>.

```
J D P T A B R E T S W H A T R
A N O I N T E D I S M I D S T
S O V L H E R W T A S N S A E
P M Z L E S G O L D A E E R K
E A N I A T N U O M P I P D E
R I E N P E I A L B P Y W I E
H D D I S R R C M E H N C U P
H E R Q X S E I O K I A C S A
F W A U Y I V P F V R H U Z W
O A G I N H O I A B E O Y A S
U L F T O S C I U R I R W P R
N K H Y Y S T N U C E N E O V
D E T A E R C B E V I D W T S
E D W I D L A R E M E Y L O H
O L Y R E B P E R F E C T N D
```

Secret Message

_____

_____

_____

_____

_____

_____

50

Heart of Stone

Ezekiel 36:25–28

<u>**Then will**</u> I **sprinkle** clean **water** upon you, and <u>**ye shall be clean**</u>: <u>**from all**</u> your **filthiness**, and from all your **idols**, will I **cleanse** you. <u>**A new heart**</u> also <u>**will I give**</u> you, and a <u>**new spirit**</u> <u>**will I put**</u> within you: and I <u>**will take**</u> **away** the **stony** heart <u>**out of your**</u> flesh, and I will give <u>**you an heart of flesh**</u>. And I will <u>**put my**</u> spirit within you, and **cause** you to **walk** in my **statutes**, and ye shall **keep** my **judgments**, and <u>**do them**</u>. And ye shall **dwell** <u>**in the land**</u> that I <u>**gave to**</u> your **fathers**; and ye shall <u>**be my**</u> **people**, and I will be <u>**your God**</u>.

```
I R E T A W I N T H E L A N D
D B Y W R H W I L L T A K E L
O Y A T U A T U P I L L I W L
L M E X O P E L K N I R P S E
S T O N Y Y F H R E S S S P W
I U O A F R O N W T S S D I D
O P W E O E Y U N E E K L R L
S A P M T O S E A T N L Y I L
G E A E U H M N U N I A E T I
D L S R O G S T A G H W S O W
L O G U D P A E I E T E H D N
A O T U A T L V L K L D A D E
D R J H S C E E E F I C L R H
F A T H E R S E E T F S L S T
Y M E B E M P Z E K O O I E L
```

Secret Message

_____

_____

_____

_____

_____

_____

51

Safe from Harm

Daniel 3:26–27

Then **Nebuchadnezzar** came near to the **mouth** of the **burning fiery furnace**, and **spake**, and said, **Shadrach, Meshach,** and **Abednego**, ye **servants** of the **most high God**, come forth, and **come hither**. Then Shadrach, Meshach, and Abednego, **came forth** of the **midst** of the **fire**. And the **princes, governors,** and **captains,** and the king's **counsellors,** being gathered **together,** saw these men, upon whose **bodies** the fire had **no power,** nor was an **hair** of their head **singed,** neither were their **coats** changed, nor the **smell of fire** had **passed** on them.

```
A B E D N E G O M I D S T W H
A P T W E R I F F O L L E M S
A R S T B G N I N R U B H R E
N I T A U M E O F T H T I E C
S N O O C S I N G E D A H U N
R C G S H A D R A C H T R Y C
O E E T A S T N A V R E S G O
L S T H D O G H G I H T S O M
L C H E N O P O W E R K I V E
E O E M E S H A C H N G S E H
S A R R Z R U D E S S A P R I
N T L E Z D I O V E R X A N T
U S X C A M E F O R T H K O H
O F I E R Y F U R N A C E R E
C A P T A I N S B O D I E S R
```

Secret Message

_____

_____

_____

_____

_____

_____

52

Den of Lions

Daniel 6:18–22

Then the king went to his **palace**, and **passed** the **night fasting**: **neither** were **instruments** of **musick brought before him**: and his **sleep** went from him. Then the king arose very **early** in the **morning**, and went in **haste** unto the **den of lions**. And when he came to the den, he **cried** with a **lamentable voice** unto **Daniel**: and the king **spake** and said to Daniel, O Daniel, **servant** of the **living** God, is thy God, whom thou **servest continually**, able to **deliver** thee from the **lions**? Then said Daniel **unto the king**, **O king**, live **for ever**. **My God** hath sent his **angel**, and hath shut the lions' **mouths**, that they have **not hurt me**.

```
P A S S E D Y W T S E V R E S
T H L A T L E K K C I S U M I
H D E I R C N N A G T D M T F
G B S A V L I L O N D D Y R O
U L E E A I A N E F I L G U R
O N I F R P N M D G L E O H E
R N T O O V U G E A N I D T V
B L I O N R A N U N N A O O E
G R S G T S E N E E T I R N R
N E V S H H I H T I E A E E S
I V N U N T E E I T T C B L L
N I D E N U R K S M I H A L E
R L F O T O E A I O R D E A E
O E C R I M H P V N U S X R P
M D X G N I T S A F G N I K O
```

Secret Message

_____

_____

_____

_____

_____

_____

53

Faithful Husband

Hosea 11:1–4

When **Israel** was a **child**, then **I loved him**, and **called** my **son** out of **Egypt**. As they called them, so **they went** from them: they **sacrificed** unto **Baalim**, and **burned incense** to **graven images**. I **taught Ephraim** also to go, taking them by their **arms**; but they **knew not** that I **healed** them. I **drew** them with **cords** of a **man**, with **bands of love**: and **I was to them** as they that **take off** the **yoke** on their **jaws**.

```
C W S H A T O N W E N K T P R
H O S M T S A C R I F I C E D
I I E T R Y O K E U T W S E D
L I D S W A J T E H E P E R O
D P H E N T S D R O C H G R O
S I L O V E D H I M F E A A D
M S A R R Y C T T O H F M M P
I R C T U R E N G O E D I I S
T A C A L L E D I R A E N L L
P E A T I W O N S D L H E A I
Y L P W Y I M A N T E H V A F
G A I E V O L F O S D N A B T
E P H R A I M H O L E S R S I
S T A U G H T N R A E L G U X
X Q M E H T O T S A W I G K B
```

Secret Message

_____

_____

_____

_____

_____

_____

54

Call to Repentance

Joel 2:11–14

And the LORD shall **utter** his **voice** before his **army**: for his camp is **very great**: for he is **strong** that **executeth his word**: for **the day of the LORD** is great and very terrible; and who can **abide** it? Therefore also now, saith the LORD, **turn ye even to me** with **all your heart**, and with **fasting**, and with **weeping**, and with **mourning**: And **rend your heart**, and not your garments, and turn unto the LORD your God: for he is gracious and merciful, **slow to anger**, and of great kindness, and **repenteth** him of **the evil**. Who knoweth if he will return and repent, and leave a **blessing** behind him; even a **meat offering** and a **drink** offering unto **the LORD your God**?

```
W M H U T T E R I G N O R T S
D O G R U O Y D R O L E H T L
C U T G R H F L E Y T X T V O
I R H N N G B U P G R E R E W
G N E D Y I O E E S A C A R T
N I E J E B P O N D E U E Y O
I N V D E L E E T R H T H G A
T G I L V E S A E O R E R R N
S B L K E S Y E T W U T U E G
A R M Y N S C I H S O H O A E
F S P A T I R T O I Y F Y T R
G O D S O N R J U H L D D G M
E N T V M G O D N I L S N R A
D R O L E H T F O Y A D E H T
M E A T O F F E R I N G R E L
```

Secret Message

_____

_____

_____

_____

_____

_____

55

Prepare to Meet Thy God

Amos 4:11–13

I have overthrown some of you, as God overthrew **So-dom** and **Gomorrah,** and ye were as a **firebrand plucked** out of the **burning:** yet have ye **not returned** unto me, saith **the LORD**. Therefore thus will I do unto thee, **O Is-rael:** and because I will do this unto thee, prepare to **meet thy God,** O Israel. For, lo, **he that formeth** the **moun-tains,** and **createth** the **wind,** and **declareth** unto man what is his **thought,** that **maketh** the **morning darkness,** and **treadeth** upon the **high places** of the **earth,** The LORD, The **God of hosts,** is **his name.**

```
M B M A K E T H E S I D D D E
O S H O V E R T H R O W N B E
R I S T U D R O L E H T A I N
N P E G E N A P B L H C R R W
I L C O E M T U E G P R B D H
N U A H E A R A U T W E E O T
G C L H A N R O I T V A R G E
D K P O I S H T F N C T I Y R
A E H N I T A T H T S E F H A
R D G O I O N D M I A T D T L
K A I M G O M O R R A H O T C
N S H H T E D A E R T E T E E
E N G A N O T R E T U R N E D
S G H I S N A M E E I N X M H
S T S O H F O D O G I H A V E
```

Secret Message

_____

_____

_____

_____

_____

_____

56

Upon Mount Zion. . .

Obadiah 15–17

For the **day of the Lord** is **near** upon all the **heathen**: as **thou hast done**, it shall be done unto **thee**: **thy reward** shall **return** upon thine **own head**. For as **ye have drunk** upon my **holy mountain**, so shall all the heathen **drink continually**, yea, they shall drink, and they shall **swallow down**, and they **shall** be as though they **had not been**. But upon **mount Zion** shall be **deliverance**, and there shall be **holiness**; and the **house** of **Jacob shall possess** their **possessions**.

```
H H D E L I V E R A N C E E O
W A M R A S W A L L O W E P H
N D D Y E D H V E N R H S O O
S N E A R T R A T E T S D S L
S O O E Y H U I L S T H E S Y
E T O L D O N R N L T O T E M
S B E S J U F T N K W S H S O
S E A M A H E T H N S A Y S U
O E N L C A T E H E V S R I N
P N L S O S A E N E H O E O T
L Y D R B T A I D T L E W N A
L S O T H D L R B O O O A S I
A K W E H O U S E O B A R D N
H I N A H N H C O N T A D D I
S N X X K E M O U N T Z I O N
```

Secret Message

_____

_____

_____

_____

_____

_____

57

Bad Choice

Jonah 1:1–4

Now the **word of the LORD came** unto **Jonah** the **son of Amittai**, saying, **Arise**, go to **Nineveh**, that **great city**, and **cry against it**; for **their wickedness** is come up **before me**. But Jonah **rose** up to **flee unto Tarshish** from the **presence** of the LORD, and went **down to Joppa**; and he **found** a **ship going** to Tarshish: so he **paid the fare** thereof, and **went** down into it, to go with them unto Tarshish from the presence of the LORD. But the LORD sent out a **great wind** into **the sea**, and there was a **mighty tempest** in the sea, so that the ship was **like** to be **broken**.

```
F L E E U N T O H R O W L A M
O T H E I R A C N P O Y I P P
U E C N E S E R P E I S K P O
N T M I G H T Y P T L H E O W
D I A T I M M A F O N O S J I
N E N R L I V G R E D E I O C
I N T E S H E A C I I T W T K
W Y H O V H C I T Y S F H N E
T C A M E E I N N I N E E W D
A V N E H W H S H N S G G O N
E W O R D O F T H E L O R D E
R E J N J O N I A K A I E H S
G T E M P E S T P O R N A E S
P A I D T H E F A R E G T A C
H E E M E R O F E B D I N I T
```

Secret Message

_____

_____

_____

_____

_____

_____

58

What God Wants

Micah 6:6-8

Wherewith shall I <u>**come before**</u> the LORD, and <u>**bow myself**</u> before the <u>**high God**</u>? shall I come before him with <u>**burnt offerings**</u>, with **calves** of <u>**a year old**</u>? Will the LORD be **pleased** with **thousands** of **rams**, or with ten thousands of <u>**rivers of oil**</u>? shall I give my **firstborn** for my **transgression**, the **fruit** of my **body** for the <u>**sin of my soul**</u>? He **hath shewed** thee, <u>**O man**</u>, what is **good**; and what doth the LORD **require** of thee, but to do **justly**, and to love **mercy**, and to **walk humbly** with thy God?

```
C A Y E A R O L D E S A E L P
B A W E R I U Q E R H I L C H
V U L E M V R S E I N U O M I
F C R V A E H N A M O S R P R
I O A N E R R G P S H E D C C
R Y M N T S O C Y A M Y E O W
S S S B B O W M Y S E L F M H
T E T H D F F B L D E B H E E
B J E M R O A F O S T M H B R
O U E U N I B G E D I U R E E
R S I I T L H H P R Y H L F W
N T S A C G E O F J I E S O I
U L N O I S S E R G S N A R T
S Y S H E W E D H A T H G E H
X K L A W T H O U S A N D S X
```

Secret Message

_____

_____

_____

_____

_____

_____

59

One Scary God

Nahum 1:2–6

God is jealous, and the LORD **revengeth**; the LORD revengeth, and is **furious**; the LORD will **take vengeance** on his **adversaries**, and he **reserveth wrath** for **his enemies**. The LORD is slow to **anger**, and **great in power**, and will not at all **acquit** the **wicked**: the LORD hath his way in the **whirlwind** and in the **storm**, and the **clouds** are the **dust** of his **feet**. He rebuketh the sea, and **maketh it dry**, and **drieth** up all the **rivers**: **Bashan** languisheth, and **Carmel**, and the **flower** of Lebanon languisheth. The **mountains quake** at him, and the hills **melt**, and the earth is burned at his **presence**, yea, the **world**, and all that dwell therein. **Who can stand** before his indignation?

```
G R E A T I N P O W E R R W H
R A W H I R L W I N D T E D S
E I S D N A D C O U H C G G D
S Y N E U P K R S R N M N O U
E R I N I E R T I A L C A D O
R D A A D M O E E E A D L I L
V T T H L R E G S H T I S S C
E I N S M P N N R E O H P J A
T H U A R E H T E G N E V E R
H T O B V E L F H S E C E A M
W E M E C Y V T O F I K E L E
R K K A C Q U I T N I H A O L
A A D V E R S A R I E S N U E
T M R E W O L F U R I O U S Q
H V E H D N A T S N A C O H W
```

Secret Message

_____

_____

_____

_____

_____

_____

60

Idols Are Dumb

Habakkuk 2:18–20

What **profiteth** the **graven image** that the **maker** thereof hath graven it; the **molten** image, and a **teacher of lies**, that the maker of his **work trusteth therein**, to make **dumb idols**? **Woe unto him** that **saith** to the **wood**, Awake; to the dumb **stone, Arise, it shall teach**! Behold, it is **laid over** with **gold** and **silver**, and there is **no breath** at all in the **midst** of it. But **the LORD** is in his **holy temple**: **let all** the **earth keep silence before** him.

```
H T R A E H T O S I L E N C E
W M H A N S N E T L O M Y L C
H B A E D P P R T E I R S E D
O S E I L F O R E H C A E T T
G E M F W O R K O V S T A A R
D R H E O B R T B F L O R L U
U M A K E R N D H E I I I L S
M O K V O U E F T E H T S H T
B E G P E R E E P O R O E P E
I H E O T N K N H E A E L T T
D B W A L A I D O V E R I D H
O D O O W D K M K T U K K N T
L H C A E T L L A H S T I C I
S N O B R E A T H G O N T A A
I H O L Y T E M P L E N X X S
```

Secret Message

_____

_____

_____

_____

_____

_____

61

A God Who Sings

Zephaniah 3:14–17

Sing, O **daughter of Zion**; **shout**, O **Israel**; be **glad** and **rejoice** with all the **heart**, O daughter of **Jerusalem**. The LORD hath **taken away** thy **judgments**, he hath **cast out** thine **enemy**: the **king of Israel**, even the LORD, is **in the midst** of thee: thou shalt **not see evil** any more. **In that day** it shall **be said** to Jerusalem, **Fear thou not**: and to Zion, Let not thine **hands** be **slack**. The LORD **thy God** in the midst of thee is **mighty**; he will **save**, he will rejoice over thee **with joy**; he will **rest in his love**, he will joy over thee with singing.

```
H E A R T O N U O H T R A E F
I K I N G O F I S R A E L J G
N N J E R U S A L E M S W U L
T D O G Y H T H A T A T S D A
H W I T H J O Y T H G I M G D
A G N I S S L O R D Y N R M I
T S D I M E H T N I A H N E R
D A U G H T E R O F Z I O N E
A C K C A L S E S C A S P T J
Y A Y E E I L D V T D L A S O
L S W M N V N E E I L O L K I
N T O W E A A N A T L V O J C
O O N A H N W S H R I E S D E
O U O M E D E A B Y S H O U T
Z T E P H B A N Y I A I H X X
```

Secret Message

_____

_____

_____

_____

_____

_____

62

Rebuilding Project

Haggai 1:3–8

Then came the **word of the LORD** by **Haggai** the **prophet**, saying, **Is it time** for you, O ye, to dwell in your **cieled houses**, and this house **lie waste**? Now therefore **thus saith** the LORD of hosts; **Consider your ways**. Ye have **sown much**, and **bring** in **little**; ye eat, but ye have **not enough**; ye **drink**, but ye are not **filled** with drink; ye **clothe** you, but there is **none warm**; and he that **earneth wages** earneth wages to put it into a **bag with holes**. Thus saith the LORD of hosts; Consider your ways. **Go up** to the **mountain**, and **bring wood**, and build the house; and I will take **pleasure** in it, and I will be glorified, saith the LORD.

```
C B W H O W N I S I T T I M E
A O R S G O V O E R H N D O A
E B N I R O F J N U S R R U R
D R A S N E A H S E O W I H N
S I U G I G H S E L W H N N E
Y N H S W D A T E A N A K G T
A G O G A I E H O A M G R I H
W W U T T E T R R L U G G M W
R O E H E F L H L D C A T H A
U O E R O N E P H I H I B F G
O D U D I G O U P O T L D I E
Y I R N G O F U T H L T E L S
M O U N T A I N G T E E L L M
W P L C I E L E D H O U S E S
P R O P H E T S A W E I L D E
```

Secret Message

_____

_____

_____

_____

_____

_____

63

Comforting Zion

Zechariah 1:14–17

So the **angel** that **communed** with me said unto me, <u>**Cry thou**</u>, saying, Thus saith the <u>**L**ORD **of hosts**</u>; I am **jealous** for **Jerusalem** and for **Zion** with a great jealousy. And I am very **sore displeased** with the **heathen** that are <u>**at ease**</u>: for I was but a little displeased, and they **helped** forward the **affliction**. Therefore thus saith the LORD; I am **returned** to Jerusalem with **mercies**: <u>**my house**</u> shall be **built** in it, saith the LORD of hosts, and a **line** shall be **stretched** forth upon Jerusalem. Cry yet, saying, <u>**Thus saith**</u> the LORD of hosts; My **cities** through **prosperity** shall yet be **spread** abroad; and the LORD shall yet **comfort** Zion, and shall yet **choose** Jerusalem.

```
E S O O H C J E A L O U S W H
S L A T K D E S A E L P S I D
A I I N S D R O C O M F O R T
E H F N T T U R E E Y S D E I
T E D D E T S H E T P R D T O
A L C E P H A O I E T Z E U E
F P I N C H L R H A Z R H R I
F E T U A H E S A F I U C N N
L D I M B P M H E G O E T E A
I L E M S I E S C H N D E D N
C M S O E A U S T S A E R N G
T G R C T O E Y R E S T T O E
I P A H H N R D R E R O S A L
O M E Y O C N P M E R C I E S
N N M T H U S S A I T H G X X
```

Secret Message

_____

_____

_____

_____

_____

_____

64

Proving God

Bring ye all the **tithes** into the **storehouse**, that there
may be **meat** in **<u>mine house</u>**, and **<u>prove me</u>** now here-
with, saith the Lord **of hosts**, if I will not open you the
windows of **heaven**, and **pour** you out a **blessing**, that
there shall not be **<u>room enough</u>** to **receive** it. And I will
rebuke the **devourer** for **<u>your sakes</u>**, and he shall not
destroy the **fruits** of your **ground**; neither shall your **vine
cast** her fruit before **<u>the time</u>** in the **field**, saith the Lord
of hosts. And all **nations** shall call you **blessed**: for ye
shall be a **delightsome land,** saith the Lord of hosts.

```
W T W B C H P R O V E M E A S
I A H L A N D E T F W A S T G
N E E E S O D R R S C Y S H R
D M S S T A R U G E A O Y G O
O A U S I I I O E N H U O S O
W R O E T T M V M F R R R I M
S E H D S S R E O A E S T H E
E C E R E L I D S N B A S E N
H E R M U A R L T A U K E A O
T I O C H O I C H H K E D V U
I V T A L P P T G E E S F E G
T E S U O H E N I M V I R N H
N A T I O N S T L H E I I R E
E V E G N I S S E L B R N R S
E E I G R O U N D G B H T E X
```

Secret Message

_____

_____

_____

_____

_____

_____

65

Prayer

Matthew 6:5–8

And when **thou prayest**, thou **shalt** not be as the **hypocrites** are: for they **love** to pray **standing** in the **synagogues** and in the **corners** of the **streets**, that they may be **seen** of men. **Verily** I say unto you, They have their **reward**. But thou, when thou prayest, **enter** into thy **closet**, and when thou hast **shut** thy **door**, pray to thy Father which is in **secret**; and thy Father which **seeth** in secret shall reward thee **openly**. But when ye pray, use not **vain repetitions**, as the **heathen** do: for they **think** that they shall be **heard** for their much **speaking**. Be not ye **therefore** like unto them: for your **Father knoweth** what things ye have **need** of, **before** ye **ask** him.

```
S W H T L A H S E D R R S S V
Y E C L O S E T I R E N R E A
N H M A V T T H E A T W E T I
A S T G E O S P E W N T N I N
G S P E A K I N G E E E R R R
O Y L A W R E S P R E R O C E
G L B E F O R E C C I O C O P
U N F U I C N E I N D F S P E
E E T O R A S K U D R E C Y T
S P T H I N K T R E A R N H I
I O S T R E E T S E E E E O T
N H E A T H E N S N H H E O I
N H E O W G N I D N A T S T O
O P T R Y L I R E V A Y A X N
X S H U T N T S E Y A R P F S
```

Secret Message

_____ _____

_____

_____

_____

_____

_____

66

The Lost Sheep

Matthew 18:10–13

Take **heed** that ye **despise** not one of these **little ones**; for I say unto you, That in **heaven** their **angels** do **always** **behold** the **face** of my **Father** which is in heaven. For the **Son of man** is **come** to **save** that which was **lost**. How **think** ye? if a man have an **hundred sheep**, and one of them be gone **astray**, doth he not **leave** the ninety and nine, and **goeth** into the **mountains**, and **seeketh** that which is **gone** astray? And if so be that he **find** it, **verily** I **say** unto you, he **rejoiceth** more of that sheep, than of the **ninety and nine** which **went not** astray.

```
H U N D R E D S H E E P W H L
E A A T H T E C I O J E R O E
A N R M O U N T A I N S S E A
T G I H D L O H E B E T S T V
O E R N I E I S C A N L H L E
E L D T D W H T A R E H T A F
T S G J S N E E T S V U E S U
N S O Y S E A N E L A D O T C
A Y N A O T E Y T E E A G C O
M A E R H V E K T N H O R Y M
F W I T H I N K E E O M N P E
O L E S I P S E D T N T O E R
N A T A A N T V L Y H I E C S
O V E R I L Y A A S S O N A N
S S H E E D X S X V D N I F Y
```

Secret Message

_____

_____

_____

_____

_____

_____

67

The Greatest Commandment

Matthew 22:34–40

But when the **Pharisees** had **heard** that he had put the **Sadducees** to **silence**, they were **gathered together**. Then one of them, which was a **lawyer**, asked him a **question, tempting** him, and **saying, Master**, which is the **great commandment** in the **law**? **Jesus** said unto him, Thou **shalt love** the <u>Lord thy God</u> with all thy **heart**, and with all thy **soul**, and with all thy **mind**. This is the **first** and great commandment. And the **second** is like unto it, Thou shalt love thy **neighbour** as **thyself**. On these two commandments **hang** all the law and the **prophets**.

```
T H Y S E L F T A E R G W H E
R U O B H G I E N R N D E W E
R D N I M E R T H I O E I S L
R A O R E L S I T G T E S E U
N S I E C A T P Y H A N G M O
P A T H E D M H E C N E L I S
W Y S T H E T A J E S U S E A
S I E E T D R R E N T H C E D
T N U G R T S I Y W E O R E D
E G Q O E G H S I D N V E N U
H T L T T H A E W D R E T E C
P N C E S O L E A M M A A N E
O D M V A E T S L A W Y E R E
R N C O M M A N D M E N T H S
P T S L X X D E R E H T A G N
```

Secret Message

_____

_____

_____

_____

_____

_____

68

The Resurrection

Matthew 28:5–10

I know that ye **seek** Jesus, which was **crucified**. He is not here: for he is **risen**. . . . **Come**, see the **place** where the **Lord** lay. And go **quickly**, and tell his **disciples** that he is risen from the dead; and, **behold**, he **goeth** before you into **Galilee**; there shall ye see him: lo, I have told you. And they **departed** quickly from the sepulchre with **fear** and **great joy**; and did **run** to bring his disciples **word**. And as they went to **tell** his disciples, behold, Jesus met them, saying, **All hail**. And they came and held him by the **feet**, and **worshipped** him. Then said **Jesus** unto them, Be not **afraid**: go tell my **brethren** that they go into Galilee, and there shall they see me.

```
N W W H E N N Q U I C K L Y G
T U O H E E A N G A E M O C O
E L R O S D F D T H F E L R E
E S D I O R E E D R O R L U T
L E R H C L U P E S E L A C H
D E L B A C K P A T O H E I S
T K O I N E W I H R Y D I F D
L D T Y L H E H D N T G R I L
I A V O E A K S E E E E P E O
A E R J S S G R H A K E D D H
H T A T N D H O B E S L E C E
L O E A M T E W L C I U L K B
L E D E E E A D R A E F S E M
A E N R F X X G J L Y C E E T
F N B G D I S C I P L E S Y J
```

Secret Message

_____

_____

_____

_____

_____

_____

69

Crowds Follow Jesus

Mark 3:7–12

But **Jesus withdrew** himself with his **disciples** to the **sea**: and a <u>**great multitude**</u> from **Galilee followed** him, and from **Judaea**, and from **Jerusalem**, and from **Idumaea**, and from beyond **Jordan**; and they about **Tyre** and **Sidon**, a great multitude, when they had heard what great things he did, came unto him. And he spake to his disciples, that a <u>**small ship**</u> should **wait** on him because of the multitude, lest they should **throng** him. For he had **healed** many; **insomuch** that they **pressed** upon him for to **touch** him, as many as had **plagues**. And **unclean spirits**, when they saw him, fell down before him, and **cried**, saying, Thou art the <u>**Son of God**</u>. And he **straitly** charged them that they should not make him **known**.

```
W H Y J E R U S A L E M P Y C
S O L O E U L D C J E S L P E
M F T R U S S N R D O L A R D
A O I D O P U N I G E R G E U
L L A A E I N S E A T N U S T
L L R N E R C R D A O A E S I
S O T T O I W N O R P E S E T
H W S E P T N L H E A L E D L
I E E L Y S A T Y R E C F O U
P D E R T T E R H E A N K G M
H S E I D U M A E A D U N F T
A L A E D H A M A N U W O O A
I W H C U O T T H L J E W N E
P R O S G A L I L E E Y N O R
I N S O M U C H W N O D I S G
```

Secret Message

_____

_____

_____

_____

_____

_____

70

The Day or Hour

Mark 13:32–37

But of that **day** and that **hour** knoweth no **man**, no, not
the **angels** which are in **heaven**, neither the **Son**, but the
Father. Take ye **heed, watch** and **pray**: for ye know not
when the **time** is. For the Son of Man is as a man taking
a far **journey**, who left his **house**, and gave **authority** to
his **servants**, and to every man his **work**, and **commanded**
the **porter** to watch. Watch ye therefore: for ye know
not when the **master** of the house **cometh**, at **even**, or at
midnight, or at the **cockcrowing**, or in the **morning**: **Lest**
coming **suddenly** he find you **sleeping**. And what I say
unto you I say unto all, Watch.

```
M W H S A T D O E R E T S A M
I S H O U S E T M H E L L O R
D D P N R V K O O M E E Y A I
N R S E E W R I L G M L L U N
I E C N E N O Y N I V C N T C
G T E O I S W A T C H O E H O
H R R N C P T D E E H M D O M
T O G A S K S N A W A E D R M
Y P R E V E C N A T H T U I A
O R U E G H H R E V A H S T N
V A U E H N A J O U R N E Y D
N Y D O E T N A R W T E H W E
I L L X H E A V E N I X S Q D
M I L E S T M F J I M N P H O
A Y L P R S L E E P I N G T Y
```

Secret Message

_____

_____

_____

_____

_____

_____

71

Good News

Mark 16:15-20

And he said unto them, **Go** ye into all the **world**, and **preach** the **gospel** to every **creature**. He that **believeth** and is **baptized** shall be **saved**; but he that believeth not shall be **damned**. And these **signs** shall **follow** them that believe; In my name shall they cast out **devils**; they shall speak with <u>**new tongues**</u>; they shall take up **serpents**; and if they **drink** any <u>**deadly thing**</u>, it shall not **hurt** them; they shall lay **hands** on the **sick**, and they shall **recover**. So then after the **Lord** had **spoken** unto them, he was **received** up into **heaven**, and sat on the <u>**right hand**</u> of **God**. And they went **forth**, and preached <u>**every where**</u>.

```
B W H Y D S E U G N O T W E N
A I D J E E R E V O C E R S S
P N U W O R L D S R E B A E U
T E G O S P E L K E H V T R H
I K E D B E L I E V E T H E I
Z O D A M N E D R D A S E H C
E P I P L T E S I B V E R W F
D S I G N S O R G E E H U Y E
T O W O L L O F H L N D T R S
P D T H G N I H T Y L D A E D
E R R M T O P R H U R T E V N
E A E I L C H T A H E G R E A
O S D A N O P E N L X X C E H
L O S I C K R X D E V I L S X
G F O R T H O D E V I E C E R
```

Secret Message

_____

_____

_____

_____

_____

_____

72

Mary's Song

Luke 1:46–54

My **soul** doth **magnify** the **Lord,** and my **spirit** hath **rejoiced** in **God** my **Saviour.** For he hath **regarded** the <u>low estate</u> of his **handmaiden:** for, behold, from henceforth all **generations** shall call me **blessed.** For he that is **mighty** hath done to me <u>**great things**</u>; and **holy** is his **name.** And his **mercy** is on them that **fear** him from generation to generation. He hath shewed **strength** with his arm; he hath **scattered** the **proud** in the imagination of their **hearts.** He hath put down the mighty from their seats, and **exalted** them of low degree. He hath **filled** the **hungry** with good things; and the **rich** he hath sent **empty** away. He hath **helped** his servant **Israel,** in remembrance of his mercy.

```
S C A T T E R E D Y T H G I M
G O W H D E T L A X E O T O P
N L U L O R D D S M H C I R A
I R Y L O W E S T A T E O T H
H O L Y A I T J N H V U E M G
T R R E T S L D O G D I E A E
T T I V I R M B E I E R O H N
A L I S R A A L B E C T R U E
E M H W I E A E S Y E E X N R
R A D D P L S S P E G Y D G A
G G E C S T T S I A N T G R T
A N L C R H R E R I L P D Y I
X I L X A A A D D E L M A R O
C F I S T R E N G T H E M A N
S Y F S H D H F D E P L E H S
```

Secret Message

_____

_____

_____

_____

_____

_____

73

Jesus' Birth

Luke 2:4-7

And **Joseph** also went up from **Galilee**, out of the city of **Nazareth**, into **Judaea**, unto the **city of David**, which is called **Bethlehem**; (because he was of the **house** and **lineage** of David:) To be **taxed** with **Mary** his espoused **wife**, being great **with child**. And so it was, that, while they were there, the **days** were **accomplished** that she should be **delivered**. And she brought forth her **firstborn son**, and **wrapped** him in **swaddling clothes**, and **laid** him in a **manger**; because there was no **room** for them in the **inn**.

```
A W H S A T R E G N A M W A S
C M A W R H Y G D E P P A R W
C S R A E P A A C T I S O N D
O F W D M E H E L H T E B H E
M I E D N S T N H E E H A N R
P R D L G O E I W L L T F I E
L S L I R J S L I T R O O M V
I T I N N L N L F A A L P P I
S B H G E A A R E E E C D T L
H O C O G G Z I I D A Y S V E
E R H E Y R A M D H D E R N D
D N T E W S R A H O U S E E B
O U I T J E E S U S J B X I R
T H W X C I T Y O F D A V I D
S O N X C C H A R D T O N X B
```

Secret Message

_____

_____

_____

_____

_____

_____

74

Shepherds in the Field

Luke 2:8–12

And there were in the same **country shepherds abid-
ing** in the **field**, keeping **watch** over their **flock** by **night**.
And, **lo**, the <u>**angel of the Lord**</u> came **upon** them, and the
glory of the Lord **shone** round **about** them: and they
were <u>**sore afraid**</u>. And the angel said unto them, <u>**Fear not**</u>:
for, **behold**, I bring you good **tidings** of great **joy**, which
shall be to <u>**all people**</u>. For unto you is **born** this day in
the **city** of **David** a **Saviour**, which is **Christ** the **Lord**.
And this shall be a **sign** unto you; Ye shall find the **babe**
wrapped in swaddling clothes, **lying** in a **manger**.

```
Y T I D I N G S W H S I G N D
N R O B D A T D A B O U T I D
H C T A W R I R D T H E V G S
H E B N P H O O E R D A S H D
A O E A U F T L E R D C I T Y
L K H R G O T E R H E E Y F O
L C O S N U C H U N D G N F M
P O L D I A R T O S H O N E Y
E L D R Y J O F I S P E P A H
O F I E L D A O V U N D T R M
P H E H B A B L A B I D I N G
L Y J P E S U E S S O L I O L
E N Y E B A B G C H R I S T O
T O H H E M A N N G E R X X R
J T I S O R E A F R A I D O Y
```

Secret Message

_____

_____

_____

_____

_____

_____

75

Jesus Calms the Storm

Luke 8:22–25

[Jesus] went into a **ship** with his **disciples**: and he said unto them, Let us go over unto the other **side** of the **lake**. And they **launched** forth. But as they **sailed** he **fell asleep**: and there came down a **storm of wind** on the lake; and they were filled with **water**, and were in **jeopardy**. And they came to him, and **awoke** him, saying, **Master**, master, we **perish**. Then he **arose**, and **rebuked** the **wind** and the **raging** of the water: and they **ceased**, and there was a **calm**. And he said unto them, Where is your **faith**? And they being **afraid** wondered, saying one to another, What **manner** of man is this! for he **commandeth** even the winds and water, and they **obey** him.

```
C O M M A N D E T H W H A T A
C S O U N T R Y G W E D N I W
R E I J E P R S U N S A N D O
T L H D E D E P I S I C I B K
M A S T E R T E P D L G E Y E
E U R S T R A R L E A Y A D V
E N E O L I W I N S G T O R W
A C B H S E N S J A A E K A L
F H U E S E U H S E C L A P L
R E K M I D N G O C F T L O H
A D E E E S D I S C I P L E S
I T D L O R M T H A O O K J F
D P I L A C E X I L X E O K C
E A S H T I A F P M A N N E R
S T O R M O F W I N D X M O C
```

Secret Message

_____

_____

_____

_____

_____

_____

76

Raising Lazarus

John 11:41–44

Then they **took** away the **stone** from the **place** where the **dead** was **laid**. And **Jesus lifted** up his **eyes**, and said, Father, I **thank** thee that thou hast heard me. And I knew that thou **hearest** me **always**: but because of the **people** which **stand** by I said it, that they may **believe** that thou hast **sent** me. And when he thus had **spoken**, he **cried** with a loud **voice**, Lazarus, <u>come forth</u>. And he that was dead came forth, bound **hand** and **foot** with **graveclothes**: and his face was **bound** about with a **napkin**. Jesus saith unto them, <u>**Loose him**</u>, and let him go.

```
E  C  I  O  V  A  S  D  E  A  D  F  T  S  G
E  Y  P  F  O  O  T  R  J  M  E  S  Y  T  R
L  U  E  S  R  N  O  A  I  I  S  A  E  A  A
I  D  O  S  E  L  N  H  A  Z  W  A  R  N  V
F  U  P  S  U  S  E  F  R  L  O  M  C  D  E
T  T  L  H  E  S  D  F  A  T  H  E  R  E  C
E  A  E  D  O  W  E  H  A  N  T  D  I  A  L
D  W  A  O  S  T  H  J  E  R  E  E  E  S  O
B  E  L  I  E  V  E  P  P  O  N  K  D  S  T
N  E  S  U  R  A  Z  A  L  O  D  F  O  M  H
I  A  N  Y  O  K  F  T  A  H  N  E  J  P  E
K  K  E  W  N  S  X  X  C  A  U  M  E  Y  S
P  O  V  A  S  C  O  M  E  F  O  R  T  H  A
A  O  H  V  O  I  C  N  D  E  B  H  A  N  D
N  T  O  N  A  T  S  E  R  A  E  H  C  N  G
```

Secret Message

_____

_____

_____

_____

_____

_____

77

Paul Sees the Light

Acts 9:3–7

And as he **journeyed**, <u>he came</u> near **Damascus**: and **suddenly** there **shined round** about him a **light** from **heaven**: And <u>he fell</u> to the **earth**, and **heard** a **voice saying** unto him, **Saul**, Saul, why **persecutest** thou me? And he said, Who <u>art thou</u>, **Lord**? And the Lord said, I am **Jesus** whom thou persecutest: it is <u>**hard for**</u> <u>**thee to**</u> **kick against** the **pricks**. And he **trembling** and **astonished** said, Lord, what wilt thou have <u>**me to do**</u>? And the Lord said unto him, **Arise**, and <u>**go into the city**</u>, and it **shall** be <u>**told thee**</u> what thou must do. And the <u>**men which**</u> journeyed with <u>**him stood**</u> **speechless**, **hearing** a voice, but **seeing** no man.

```
J K G N I E E S T H G I L W N
G O I N T O T H E C I T Y H E
Y S U C I S D F A A D I D S V
A U A R K R E R S R O U N D A
H H S U N L A T O L D T H E E
I C U S L E O E U L T F S S H
M I S U L N Y J H C R S O I S
S H E C I O V E O U E R N R K
T W J S H A L L D L M S A A C
O N H A D E N I H S B E R M I
O E E M E M A C E H L Y T E R
D M A A T H E E T O I T T T P
O D R D A E S A Y I N G H O M
A T D S P T S N I A G A O D C
H U S S U D D E N L Y X U O X
```

Secret Message

_____

_____

_____

_____

_____

_____

78

Who Can Be against Us?

Romans 8:35–39

Who **shall separate** us from the love of **Christ**? shall **tribulation**, or **distress**, or **persecution**, or **famine**, or **nakedness**, or **peril**, or **sword**? As it is **written**, For thy sake we are **killed** all the day long; we are **accounted** as **sheep** for the **slaughter**. Nay, in all these things we are more than **conquerors through** him that **loved** us. For I am **persuaded**, that **neither death**, nor life, nor **angels**, nor **principalities**, nor **powers**, nor things **present**, nor things to come, nor **height**, nor **depth**, nor any other **creature**, shall be able to separate us from the <u>**love of God**</u>, which is in Christ **Jesus** our **Lord**.

```
S S C W S L A U G H T E R H J
F E R O E R S S E R T S I D E
L A I E N E D I I A N G E L S
D O M T W Q P B R A D A R L U
N P R I I O U A U O T E L L S
N O R D N L P E G H H I H A C
A T I E A E A F R T P E E H S
K H N T S T O P I O I E R S N
E R I N U E D E I G R I U D T
D O K U V C N E H C S S T O G
N U I O O A E T V T N F A T H
E G L C E R V S I O S I E I T
S H L C T S W O R D L I R E P
S I E A W R I T T E N N C P E
G R D E D A U S R E P O M E D
```

Secret Message

_____

_____

_____

_____

_____

_____

79

Embrace Hope

Romans 15:13-16

Now the God of **hope** fill you with all joy and **peace** in **believing**, that ye may **abound** in hope, **through** the **power** of the **Holy Ghost**. And I **myself** also am **persuaded** of you, my **brethren**, that ye also are **full** of **goodness**, **filled** with all **knowledge**, able also to **admonish** one **another**. **Nevertheless**, brethren, I **have written** the **more boldly** unto you in some sort, as **putting** you in mind, because of the **grace** that is **given** to me of God, that I **should** be the minister of **Jesus Christ** to the **Gentiles, ministering** the **gospel** of God, that the **offering** up of the Gentiles **might** be **acceptable**, being **sanctified** by the Holy Ghost.

```
S W H A A D M O N I S H H R M
T S I R H C T F W E O A E I S
G N E G R A C E L R V H N H S
O S E L I T N E G E T I O K E
S A D T E R O M P O S U G D N
P B R E T H R E N T L Y I B D
E O D G I I T A E D A P M E O
L U W D O F R R T D E B D L O
E N R E G F I W E A E A L I G
T D P L R N F T C V U L Y E L
G O S W G T I E C S E I L V L
H G U O R H T T R N U N D I U
O S S N F G O E T I A U L N F
S L E K F I P L I U N S O G L
T L J F O M R P Y A P G B U L
```

Secret Message

_____

_____

_____

_____

_____

_____

80

First Importance

1 Corinthians 15:3–8

For I **delivered** unto you **first** of all that which I also **received**, how that **Christ died <u>for our sins</u> according** to the **scriptures**; and that <u>**he was**</u> buried, and that <u>**he rose again**</u> the <u>**third day**</u> according to the scriptures: and that he <u>**was seen**</u> of **Cephas, then** of the **twelve**: After that, he was seen of **above <u>five hundred</u> brethren** at **once**; of **whom** the **greater <u>part remain</u>** unto this **present**, but **some** are **fallen asleep**. After that, he was seen of **James**; then **<u>of all the</u> apostles**. And last of all he was seen of me also, as of <u>**one born**</u> out of **<u>due time</u>**.

```
D N E L L A F W H J A M E S P
E E H T L L A F O F S Y O R D
I R R O E E E S O G L P E H A
R H U D L M M R N E E S S A W
U T S D N H O I O N E B O R N
B E S C E U D S T N P A T Y H
S R E W R R H R T E C W H A S
E B A S O I E E E D U E I R A
L S I C T T P V V V I D R E G
T N C H A C L T I I O E D C A
S A E E E E H L U L F B D E I
O T R P W P A R T R E M A I N
P G H T E T S R I F E D Y V A
A A S E T H E R O S E S O E F
S T H E N A P O S T T L E D S
```

Secret Message

_____

_____

_____

_____

_____

_____

81

Herald of Hope

2 Corinthians 5:17–20

Therefore if any man **be in Christ**, he is a new **creature**: old **things are** passed away; behold, **all things** are **become new**. And all things **are of** God, who hath **reconciled us** to **himself** by **Jesus** Christ, and hath **given** to us the **ministry** of **reconciliation**; to wit, that God was in Christ, **reconciling** the **world** unto himself, not **imputing their trespasses** unto **them**; and hath **committed** unto us the word of reconciliation. Now then we are **ambassadors** for Christ, as **though** God did **beseech** you by us: we **pray you** in **Christ's stead**, be ye reconciled to God.

```
R W T H I N G S A R E H R W O
R E E S P O U R P T E E E T S
F R C D I S T R O P C N C R T
A O R O E R A U L O E A O E S
B F E J N Y H O N M U D N S I
T E A R Y C B C O T A L C P R
T R T O A E I C N S T R I A H
H E U H S L E L S I H O L S C
O H R E E B F A I H E W I S E
U T E D N I B L C N M B A E D
G C U E O M R R E I G N T S A
H S V S A T Y R T S I N I M E
H I I S A D E T T I M M O C T
G N Y A W A A L L T H I N G S
S I M P U T I N G D L O H E B
```

Secret Message

_____

_____

_____

_____

_____

_____

82

Abundant Harvest

Galatians 6:6–10

<u>Let him</u> that is **taught** in the **word communicate** unto him that **teacheth** in all good **things**. <u>Be not</u> **deceived**; <u>God is not</u> mocked: for **whatsoever** <u>a man</u> **soweth**, that **shall** <u>he also</u> reap. For he that soweth to <u>his flesh</u> shall of the <u>flesh reap</u> **corruption**; but he that soweth to the **Spirit** shall of the Spirit <u>reap life</u> everlasting. And let us not be **weary** in **well doing**: for in due **season** we shall reap, if we <u>faint not</u>. As we have therefore **opportunity**, let us <u>do good</u> unto <u>all men</u>, **especially** unto **them** who are of the **household** <u>of faith</u>.

```
W A H A L L M E N W E A R Y O
S M S G N I H T E E M N S P D
P A E R H S E L F I O H R E L
H N H T E R L I H I C T E S O
T T E E T V S S T C K E A P H
S L I V A A E P R I E W P E E
G E E A E L U O I S D O L C S
H N A D F R S G S R R S I I U
T O I S R F L O H T I U F A O
E T I O O O O A U T A T E L H
H H C A D N W N S B S H A L L
C O M M U N I C A T E B W Y A
A B E N O T D E C E I V E D F
E H A T Y H G O D I S N O T E
T O N T N I A F R D O O G O D
```

Secret Message

_____

_____

_____

_____

_____

83

Rich in Mercy

Ephesians 2:6–10

And hath <u>**raised us**</u> up <u>**together**</u>, and <u>**made us**</u> sit together in **heavenly places** in **Christ Jesus**: That in the
<u>**ages to**</u> <u>**come he**</u> **might** shew the **exceeding riches** of his
grace in his **kindness toward** us **through** Christ Jesus.
<u>**For by grace are ye saved**</u> through **faith**; and <u>**that not of**</u>
yourselves: <u>**it is the gift of God**</u>: not of **works**, lest any
man **should boast**. For we are his **workmanship, created**
in Christ Jesus unto **good** works, **which** God hath **before**
ordained that we should **walk** in **them**.

```
W  H  C  I  H  W  H  E  D  A  H  T  I  A  F
D  E  N  I  A  D  R  O  R  T  H  G  I  M  T
N  S  U  L  M  C  G  H  E  A  V  E  N  L  Y
B  U  K  Y  H  F  O  R  T  R  E  B  E  R  B
O  D  D  R  O  T  W  N  E  O  O  C  E  S  R
A  E  I  T  S  U  O  J  X  H  W  F  A  C  O
S  S  F  E  C  T  R  E  C  M  T  A  E  R  F
T  I  G  W  O  R  K  S  E  R  A  E  R  B  G
G  A  I  F  M  B  M  U  E  P  D  D  G  D  E
E  R  S  F  E  A  A  S  D  L  E  O  E  O  H
D  L  U  O  H  S  N  I  I  A  V  T  O  U  T
R  I  C  H  E  S  S  T  N  C  A  E  T  G  S
T  H  R  O  U  G  H  H  G  E  S  H  S  H  I
S  S  E  N  D  N  I  K  R  S  E  O  P  E  T
A  N  D  B  A  P  P  C  T  M  Y  I  S  M  I
```

Secret Message

_____

_____

_____

_____

_____

_____

84

Rejoice Evermore

Philippians 4:4–8

Rejoice in the Lord **always**: and again I say, Rejoice. Let your **moderation** be **known** unto all men. The **Lord** is at hand. Be **careful** for **nothing**; but in every thing by **prayer** and **supplication** with **thanksgiving** let your **requests** be made known unto God. And the **peace** of God, which **passeth** all **understanding**, shall keep your **hearts** and **minds through Christ Jesus. Finally, brethren, whatsoever things** are **true**, whatsoever things are **honest**, whatsoever things are **just**, whatsoever things are **pure**, whatsoever things are **lovely**, whatsoever things are of **good report**; if there **be any** virtue, and if there be any **praise, think** on these things.

```
W T H A C H R I S T J P Y N T
T P R A I S E Y W U M L U E O
H N M O W H A T S O E V E R A
R T O N P W P T D V G N R H E
O S H I L E F E O H O W E T R
U D A A T I R L Y T O O Q E E
G N I D N A T S R E D N U R V
H I D A T K C H C S U K E B I
B M L I Y J S I E S T R S S R
H L O E E R O G L A G I T K T
Y N V S P J E R I P R N S N U
S L U F E R A C D V P T I I E
I S P R A Y E R D R I U S H E
N E A R C G N I H T O N S T T
P Y N A E B H I L I P L G P I
```

Secret Message

_____

_____

_____

_____

_____

_____

85

Clothed with Kindness

Colossians 3:11–15

Where there is **neither Greek** nor Jew, circumcision nor **uncircumcision, Barbarian, Scythian, bond** nor **free**: but **Christ** is all, and in all. Put on therefore, as the **elect** of God, **holy** and **beloved, bowels** of **mercies, kindness, humbleness** of mind, **meekness, longsuffering; forbearing** one **another**, and **forgiving** one another, if any man have a **quarrel** against any: even as Christ **forgave** you, so also do ye. And above all these **things** put on **charity**, which is the bond of **perfectness**. And let the **peace** of God **rule** in **your hearts**, to the which also ye are **called** in one **body**; and be ye **thankful**.

S D U S C Y T H I A N S S P E
G A N O T H E R P E A S G C H
P N C O G R R E H T I E N S F
H E I O B R A U E H R N I L O
E D R R B C E E M A A K H E R
W L C F E I R E H N B E T H G
T C U O E F R H K K R E U N A
G H M R Q C F B R F A M I A V
R R C B I U T U E U B V C C E
U I I E E S A N S L I E B A A
O S S A W H E R E G O H O L Y
Y T I R A H C N R S N V W L D
S O O I N E E O D E S O E E O
W I N N T S F T C E L E L D B
H W H G S S E N D N I K S A T

Secret Message

_____

_____

_____

_____

_____

86

Rest Assured

1 Thessalonians 4:15–17

For **this <u>we say</u> <u>unto you</u> <u>by the word</u>** of the Lord, **that** we **which** are **<u>alive and remain</u>** unto the **coming** of the Lord **<u>shall not</u> prevent them** which **<u>are asleep</u>**. For the Lord **himself** shall **descend from heaven** with a **shout**, with the **voice** of the **archangel**, and with the **<u>trump of God</u>**: and the **dead** in **Christ** shall **<u>rise first</u>**: **Then** we which **<u>are alive</u>** and remain shall be **<u>caught up</u> together** with them **<u>in the clouds</u>**, to **meet** the Lord **<u>in the air</u>**: and so shall we ever be **<u>with the Lord</u>**.

```
N D E A D W H H C I H W O S T
E I R H O R I S E F I R S T U
U N A O C A U G H T U P T S O
E T I M W N W C H T M E H T H
R H R T E E M T O N L L A H S
I E H U S R H E S M U S T P L
A C H A M E D T D O I T H E N
E L Y T L P A N Y N L N G E F
H O P O E H O O A B E N G L R
T U R R E G T F O E A C E S O
N D N A E N O E G H V S S A M
I S V I U V C T C O M I A E W
A E V I L A E R A I D H L R D
N S A S S A A N H U O T L A T
E D B C H R I S T Y A V M O B
```

Secret Message

_____

_____

_____

_____

_____

_____

87

God Is Just

2 Thessalonians 1:5–9

Which is a **manifest token** of the **righteous judgment** of God, that ye may be **counted worthy** of the **kingdom** of God, for which ye also **suffer: Seeing** it is a righteous **thing** with God to **recompense tribulation** to them that trouble you; and to you who are **troubled** rest with us, when the **Lord Jesus shall** be **revealed** from **heaven** with his **mighty angels**, in **flaming** fire **taking vengeance** on them that **know** not God, and that **obey** not the **gospel** of our Lord Jesus **Christ**: who shall be **punished** with **everlasting destruction** from the **presence** of the Lord, and from the **glory** of his **power**.

```
E W G L O R Y R F R E W O P H
A V N B T H D D E L B U O R T
S A E E T O R C L F A E S E H
U Y N R V O N R L P F M A S I
S U O G L A T I A D D U I E N
E W L S E A E G H E A Y S N G
J S A G K L S H S H T B O C G
M A N I F E S T U S N T C E T
H E N E E O R E I I E T H G K
V G S I P U E O W N M O R O I
W O N K C M H U O U G K I S N
W G O T U L O S D P D E S P G
N M I G H T Y C C O U N T E D
O O D E L A E V E R J T W L O
N O I T A L U B I R T O R K M
```

Secret Message

_____

_____

_____

_____

_____

_____

88

Remain Resolute

1 Timothy 6:11–14

But thou, O man of God, **flee** these **things**; and **follow** after **righteousness, godliness, faith, love, patience, meekness. Fight** the **good** fight of faith, lay **hold** on **eternal life,** whereunto thou art also **called,** and hast professed a good **profession** before many **witnesses.** I give thee **charge** in the **sight** of God, who **quickeneth** all things, and before **Christ Jesus,** who before **Pontius Pilate witnessed** a good **confession;** that thou **keep** this **commandment without spot, unrebukable,** until the **appearing** of our **Lord** Jesus Christ.

```
I N G N I R A E P P A E W J H
A T P A T I E N C E W T A E Y
E V O L C G O D L I N E S S D
F L E E H H O L D O P R I U E
C S B T D T A P I R H N G S A
O O I A H E F R O F T A H U S
N A M I K O L F G S E L T S L
F C N M L U E L E E N C E U A
E G H L A S B S A L E N T I L
S T O R S N S E T C K D U T T
S W A I I E D O R E C I O N T
I M O L N S P M E N I O H O H
O N O T I S T M E T U H T P G
N R I Y H P E E K N Q I I S I
D W S O D E S S E N T I W N F
```

Secret Message

_____

_____

_____

_____

_____

_____

89

A Life of Faith

2 Timothy 4:5–8

But **watch** thou in all **things, endure afflictions**, do the **work** of an **evangelist**, make full **proof** of thy **ministry**. For <u>**I am now**</u> **ready** to be **offered**, and the **time** of my **departure** <u>**is at hand**</u>. I have **fought** a **good fight**, I have **finished** <u>**my course**</u>, I have <u>**kept the faith**</u>: **Henceforth** there is <u>**laid up**</u> for me a **crown** of **righteousness**, which the **Lord**, the righteous **judge, shall** <u>**give me**</u> <u>**at that day**</u>: and <u>**not to me**</u> **only,** but unto all them also that **love** his **appearing**.

```
W W L W H E D N A H T A S I S
G O O D A J N A T E D P I D S
T P R N U T A D M U K P L Y E
A H D D M Y C O U R S E D T N
T F G E L A T H O R L A L T S
T E F U I T I W M A E R D H U
H S G L O L O T I R E I E H O
A Y I N I F L D T R O N H Y E
T L V L E C U A U T C G S R T
D I E K E P T T H E F A I T H
A N M T N G R I F S Y T N S G
Y W E E O A N O O L M H I I I
F O O R P G R A N N A G F N R
N R D E S T L O V E S I E I S
P C D I H S D E R E F F O M E
```

Secret Message

_____

_____

_____

_____

_____

90

Worthy Standard

2 Timothy 3:14–17

But **continue thou** in the **things which** thou hast **learned** and hast **been assured** of, **knowing** of **whom** thou hast learned **them**; and that from a **child** thou hast **known** the **holy scriptures**, which are able to **make** thee **wise** unto **salvation through faith** which is in **Christ Jesus**. All scripture is **given** by **inspiration** of God, and is **profitable** for **doctrine**, for **reproof**, for **correction**, for **instruction** in **righteousness**: that the man of God may be **perfect**, **thoroughly furnished** unto all **good works**.

```
S A L V A T I O N E R T H U E
U S F H H L E A R N E D A O T
S I E I C T H E P I P O R H H
E O N N O I T C E R R O C T O
J G F S S T H I R T O G I P R
S S W P T U R W F C O A R M O
K O E I T R O H E O F O Y D U
R W U R S A U E C D F H E S G
O B N A U E G C T I C H O N H
W E I T O T H F T H S H I L L
K E T I M W P A R I G W I H Y
A N N O A T B I N N O I H L A
T I O N K L S R R N O N R O D
N A C W E T U L K C I T H E M
G I V E N F D E R U S S A T Y
```

Secret Message

_____

_____

_____

_____

_____

_____

91

Relentlessly Seeking Righteousness

Titus 2:11–15

For the **grace** of God that **bringeth salvation** hath appeared to all men, **teaching** us that, **denying ungodliness** and **worldly lusts**, we should live **soberly, righteously,** and **godly,** in this **present** world; looking for that **blessed** hope, and the **glorious appearing** of the **great** God and our **Saviour Jesus Christ**; who gave **himself** for us, that he **might redeem** us from all **iniquity**, and **purify** unto himself a **peculiar people, zealous** of good **works**. These things **speak**, and **exhort**, and **rebuke** with all **authority**. Let no man **despise** thee.

```
E X H O R T R U O I V A S D P
K S P A U Y L R E B O S E L U
U Z I W A S W Y R G E N Y I R
B Y E P T S L I N N Y A T G I
E C L A S D A T I I L P I O F
R T H S L E I L N H D P U T Y
U S W R U O D G V C O E Q T H
G L O R I O U S O A G A I W B
R W T A G S E S S E T R N R L
A O N N U M T T P T O I I W E
C H U S E S S E H H H N O A S
E T E E U S O P T G G I N S S
S J D L L P E U E E I A I N E
P E C U L I A R T A E R G M D
R F L E S M I H P S K R O W D
```

Secret Message

_____

_____

_____

_____

_____

_____

92

Paul's Plea

Philemon 15–19

For **perhaps** he **therefore departed** for a **season**, that **thou shouldest receive** him for ever; not now as a **servant**, but **above** a servant, a **brother beloved**, **specially** to me, but how <u>**much more**</u> unto thee, <u>**both in the**</u> flesh, and in <u>**the Lord**</u>? If thou count me therefore a **partner**, receive <u>**him as**</u> **myself**. If he hath **wronged** thee, or **oweth** thee **ought**, put that on mine **account**; I **Paul** have **written** it with <u>**mine own**</u> hand, I <u>**will repay**</u> it: **albeit** I do not say to thee how thou **owest** unto me **even thine** <u>**own self**</u> besides.

```
Y S E D I S E B B E L O V E D
W L N R E H T O R B O W E S T
H A L A P G T N A V R E S A T
H W S A L H N A S C T T H E N
A O U M I B S O T E C H O D W
N L F N E C E H R H W O R T R
W H T E V E E I O W I O U D I
O H H S I R H P T U L N E N T
E L G A E O I A S E L T E F T
N V U F C M M R H V R D E L E
I B O E E H A T I A E N E E N
M R G B R C S N P R P E T S U
E V E N A U P E R H A P S N T
F L E S Y M D R L R Y N E W D
T O P H I L E M O F N T H O U
```

Secret Message

_____

_____

_____

_____

_____

_____

93

Persistence Triumphs

Hebrews 12:1–3

Wherefore seeing we also are **compassed** about with so **great** a **cloud** of witnesses, let us lay **aside every weight**, and the sin which doth so **easily <u>beset us</u>**, and **<u>let us run</u>** with **patience** the **race** that is set before us, **looking** unto **Jesus** the **author** and **finisher** of <u>**our faith**</u>; who for the joy that was set before him **endured** the **cross, despising** the **shame,** and is set down at the <u>**right hand**</u> of the **throne** of God. For **consider** him that endured such **contradiction** of **sinners against himself,** lest ye be **wearied** and **faint** in **your minds.**

```
I R M N C T T H R O N E D F I
D W O I O S U T E S E B E A M
E E H H N Y L I S A E E S I G
W A S E T D P A A A S C P N T
D E S S R U S F H G O N I T J
W U A I A E A R S D A E S W E
E H O R D P F U S I E I I D S
N I D L I E M O O S G T N O U
D M R A C E G O R T N A G S S
U S D S T N D P C E H P E I T
R E H S I N I F S T Y G N A S
E L K K O T O S H A R N I H T
D F O H N E E G F E E U A E A
T O C O N S I D E R V M O H W
L E T U S R U N S G E E R Y S
```

Secret Message

_____

_____

_____

_____

_____

_____

94

Genuine Religion

James 2:12–17

So **speak** ye, and so do, as they that **shall** be **judged** by the law of **liberty**. For he shall have **judgment without mercy**, that hath **shewed** no mercy; and mercy **rejoiceth against** judgment. What doth it **profit**, my **brethren**, **though** a man say he hath **faith**, and have not **works**? can faith save him? If a **brother** or **sister** be **naked**, and **destitute** of **daily food**, and one of you say unto them, **Depart** in **peace**, be ye **warmed** and **filled**; **notwithstanding** ye give them not **those things** which are **needful** to the **body**; what doth it profit? **Even** so faith, if it hath not works, is **dead, being alone**.

```
W W H A T P A R T O J F T T G
A T H E W I T H O U T I B N Y
R K R S H E W E D O F Y I L D
M Y A A Y I E G B O T D I S A
E C A E P D M V R R N A K E D
D T L I P E O P E A D T T S E
R L U F N S D B T N E T M O A
E E E T I M I S H L Y H F H D
H B J S I L H E R U C O O T R
T B T O S T L U E F R U O T B
O E O H I A S E N D E G D U J
R S A W I C T E D E M H S G R
B L T E A N E T D E N O L A T
L O B E I N G T S N I A G A H
N I N W O R K S H T I A F G S
```

Secret Message

_____

_____

_____

_____

_____

_____

95

Stand Firm

1 Peter 5:8–11

Be **sober**, be **vigilant**; **because** your **adversary** the **devil**, as a **roaring lion**, **walketh** about, **seeking whom** he may **devour**: whom **resist stedfast** in the **faith**, **knowing** that the same **afflictions** are **accomplished** in your **brethren** that are in the **world**. But the God of all **grace**, who hath **called** us **unto** his **eternal glory** by **Christ Jesus**, after that ye have **suffered** a **while**, make you **perfect**, **stablish**, **strengthen**, **settle** you. To him be glory and **dominion** for ever and ever. **Amen**.

```
T K T A N O I N I M O D P E T
S N S U F F E R E D E L I H W
I O A E R F E S G H T I A F A
R W F L Y S L S S R T H E Y A
H I D A I H S I L B A T S M R
C N E S E G L A C A S C E H O
H G T L L P I D Y T N N E J A
T T S O M D E V R N I G K E I
E O R O E L N E E U N O I S A
K Y C V L N N R T I O T N U D
L C I A T G H S R E W V G S H
A L C W T T A A P E R F E C T
W I H H E W O R L D B N T D K
I O E R S R N Y D O F O A P E
M N B E C A U S E O P L S L E
```

Secret Message

_____

_____

_____

_____

_____

_____

96

The Lord Is Patient

2 Peter 3:8–10

But, **beloved**, be not **ignorant** of this <u>**one thing**</u>, that one day is with the Lord as a **thousand years**, and a thousand years as <u>**one day**</u>. The Lord is <u>**not slack**</u> **concerning** his **promise**, as some men **count slackness**; but is **longsuffering** to <u>**us-ward**</u>, not **willing** that <u>**any should**</u> perish, but that <u>**all should**</u> come to **repentance**. But the <u>**day of the**</u> Lord will come as a **thief** in the **night**; in the which the **heavens shall** <u>**pass away**</u> with a **great noise**, and the **elements** shall melt with **fervent heat**, the **earth** also and the **works** that are therein shall be **burned** up.

```
T N U O C W H S A T T D G O E
D N A S U O H T T S H N P E T
O N E T H I N G E N I D R S A
Y S C T P S D C G R E A T S O
F D E N R U B R E V F M S F P
E R S A O O D F O R A E E E F
T H E R M N F L E L N E R L L
A Y S O I U E P U K Y I G T E
S S I N S B E D C O S S N H H
H K O G E N H A A H H U I G T
A R N I T V L E T Y O S L I F
L O P A S S A W A Y U W L N O
L W N F E R V E N T L A I L Y
K C A L S T O N H D D R W A A
E A R T H Y W I L L A D S K D
```

Secret Message

_____

_____

_____

_____

_____

_____

97

Walk in the Light

1 John 1:5–9

This then is the **message** which we have **heard** of **him**, and **declare** unto **you**, that <u>**God is light**</u>, and in him is <u>**no darkness**</u> at all. If we **say** that we have **fellowship** with him, and walk in darkness, we **lie**, and do not the **truth**: But if we <u>**walk in the light**</u>, as he is in the light, we **have** fellowship one with **another**, and the **blood** of **Jesus Christ** his **Son cleanseth** us from all **sin**. If we say that we have no sin, we **deceive ourselves**, and the truth is not in us. If we **confess** our sins, he is **faithful** and **just** to **forgive** us our **sins**, and to cleanse us **from** all **unrighteousness**.

```
S A Y H F A I T H F U L O T W
M A C O N F E S S N N Y H C H
A T S U S E J P T E R G R S A
T S T R U T H P E V I G R O F
H I P S E A Y O U L G R I S D
G R D E C E I V E N H N I T E
I H H L E N E H O W T N T E C
L C S V T A T D M E E N R M L
S H T E S N A E L C O T E I A
I B O S I R O K O F U S H H R
D F I K K D H S I N S H T M E
O R L N O E T S T A N A O O J
G A E O A S O H G N É V N R S
W S L R U X X E I L S E A F O
S B D J F E L L O W S H I P N
```

Secret Message

_____

_____

_____

_____

_____

_____

98

Love One Another

1 John 4:7–12

Beloved, let us <u>**love one another**</u>: for love is of God; and every one that **loveth** is **born** of God, and **knoweth** God. He that loveth not knoweth not God; for <u>**God is love**</u>. In this was **manifested** the love of God **toward** us, **because** that God sent his **only begotten** Son into the **world**, that we **might live through** him. **Herein** is love, not that we loved God, but that he loved us, and <u>**sent his Son**</u> to be the **propitiation** for our sins. Beloved, if God so loved us, we **ought also** to love one **another**. No **man hath** seen God at any **time**. If we love one another, God **dwelleth** in us, and his love is **perfected** in us.

```
D E T C E F R E P W H I N L C
H S F O U W O R L D R B O O O
T U H A T H K S O F T V S H E
H A M A N I F E S T E D S V E
G C A N I B I B E O T L I T E
U E N O E C O M N O T L H H N
O B T T R A I E W H I A T R N
T B H H E T A A G E W L N O N
O E R E H N R I D B E S E U E
G L I R O D M O N L Y O S G T
N O I T A I T I P O R P N H T
N V H I N G I N T V H E I R O
F E I R S K N O W E T H T V G
R D E D W E L L E T H R S E E
E V O L S I D O G H X N R O B
```

Secret Message

_____

_____

_____

_____

_____

_____

99

Build on Faith

Jude 20–25

But ye, **beloved**, building up **yourselves** on your most <u>**holy faith**</u>, praying in the <u>**Holy Ghost**</u>, keep **yourselves** in the **love** of God, looking for the **mercy** of our **Lord** Jesus **Christ** unto <u>**eternal life**</u>. And of some have **compassion**, making a **difference**: and others save with **fear**, pulling them **out** of the **fire**; hating even the **garment** spotted by the **flesh**. Now unto him that is able to keep you from **falling**, and to **present** you **faultless** before the **presence** of his glory with <u>**exceeding joy**</u>, to the only wise God our **Saviour**, be **glory** and **majesty**, **dominion** and **power**, both <u>**now and ever**</u>. **Amen**.

D I F F E R E N C E B W H A R
O U T T M E R C Y T E W O O E
L D N T A R E W O P L E S E V
R A E F J T A M D R O L X E E
E N M S E R I F T T V C C I D
F P R E S E N C E N E O H S N
I H A V T T A H I E D M O S A
L O G L Y E M R D S S P L E W
L L A E R E E I O E F A Y L O
A Y G S N A N S M R L S G T N
N F L R M G E T I P E S H L D
R A O U J I N J N U S I O U D
E I R O E S L E I T H O S A T
T T Y Y S A V I O U R N T F E
E H R F A L L I N G X E V O L

Secret Message

_____

_____

_____

_____

_____

_____

100

Alpha and Omega

Revelation 1:9–11

I **John, who** also am your **brother**, and **companion** in **tribulation**, and in the **kingdom** and **patience** of **Jesus Christ**, was in the **isle** that is called **Patmos**, for the <u>**word of God**</u>, and for the **testimony** of Jesus Christ. I was in the **Spirit** on the **Lord**'s **day**, and heard behind me a <u>**great voice**</u>, as of a **trumpet**, saying, I am **Alpha** and **Omega**, the **first** and the **last**: and, What thou **seest**, write in a **book**, and **send** it unto the <u>**seven churches**</u> which are in **Asia**; unto **Ephesus**, and unto **Smyrna**, and unto Pergamos, and unto Thyatira, and unto Sardis, and unto Philadelphia, and unto Laodicea.

```
J O H N W A D O G F O D R O W
E H A T M H Y M T S M Y R N A
S H I C E P H E S U S A T L S
U C E R E L A G T A K R E U P
S R C E A A P A S P I E S A I
R S N O S I Y I N B N R T E R
V O E E M A A T U L G A I T I
T M I R D P S L E I D C M E T
O T T E N A A S L T O H O P W
E A A H L T L N S F M R N M S
S P P T I T H C I H A I Y U E
E B O O K L O R D O P S T R N
E W N R E F I R S T N T R T D
S H X B X E C I O V T A E R G
T O S E V E N C H U R C H E S
```

Secret Message

_____

_____

_____

_____

_____

_____

101

The End of the Book

Revelation 22:18–21

For I **testify** unto <u>**every man**</u> that <u>**heareth the words**</u> of the **prophecy** of <u>**this book**</u>, If <u>**any man**</u> shall <u>**add unto**</u> these things, **God** shall add unto him the **plagues** that are **written** in this book: And if any man shall <u>**take away from**</u> the words of the book of this prophecy, God shall take away <u>**his part**</u> out of <u>**the book of life**</u>, and out of the **holy city**, and from the things which are written in this book. He which **testifieth** these things **saith, Surely <u>I come</u>** quickly. **Amen.** <u>**Even so, come**</u>, **Lord Jesus**. The **grace** of our Lord Jesus **Christ** be with <u>**you all**</u>. Amen.

```
W  S  U  S  E  J  T  R  A  P  S  I  H  H  P
E  T  O  D  R  E  C  C  M  E  G  T  I  L  R
F  E  H  R  G  W  H  V  E  E  E  R  A  D  O
I  S  T  O  H  E  R  R  N  I  E  G  A  I  P
L  T  D  W  L  V  I  I  F  E  U  L  T  C  H
F  I  A  E  E  Y  S  I  T  E  T  H  I  O  E
O  F  O  H  N  V  T  O  S  T  I  F  J  M  C
K  Y  E  T  S  S  E  U  S  S  E  C  Y  E  Y
O  H  R  H  E  I  S  R  B  T  A  N  O  S  L
O  N  Y  T  I  C  D  O  Y  R  A  E  U  U  K
B  E  V  E  N  S  O  C  O  M  E  C  A  R  C
E  O  R  R  D  K  E  D  Y  I  A  L  L  E  I
H  T  S  A  I  T  H  N  F  O  O  N  L  L  U
T  A  K  E  A  W  A  Y  F  R  O  M  R  Y  Q
U  S  T  H  O  D  A  D  D  U  N  T  O  A  Y
```

Secret Message

_____

_____

_____

_____

_____

Puzzle 1

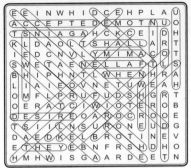

In which place did Cain live
after being driven from his garden?

The land of Nod (Genesis 4:16)

Puzzle 2

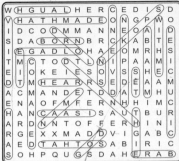

Where did God command Abraham to take
Isaac and then offer him as a burnt offering?

The land of Moriah (Genesis 22:2)

Puzzle 3

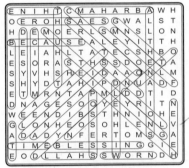

Who was the son that Abraham
did not withhold from God?

Isaac (Genesis 22:2)

Puzzle 4

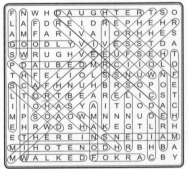

Who did Pharaoh's daughter
pay to nurse the baby?

The child's mother (Exodus 2:7–9)

Puzzle 5

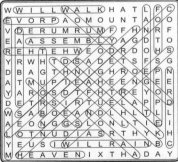

What amount of food was
gathered on the sixth day?

Twice as much (Exodus 16:5)

Puzzle 6

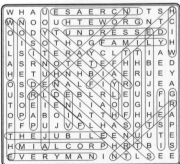

What sound declared
the Year of Jubilee?

A trumpet sound (Leviticus 25:9)

Puzzle 7

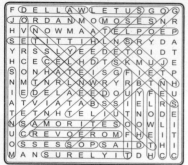

For how many days did the
men spy out the land?

Forty (Numbers 13:25)

Puzzle 8

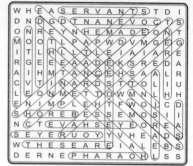

What did not wear out
while in the wilderness?

Clothes and shoes (Deuteronomy 29:5)

Puzzle 9

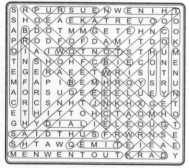

What method did the spies
use to get away?

A cord through a window (Joshua 2:15)

Puzzle 10

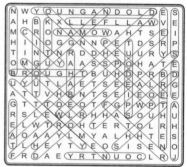

What sign did Rahab leave to
show her loyalty to Israel?

A scarlet thread (Joshua 2:21)

Puzzle 11

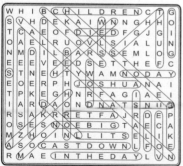

Which king of Jerusalem led
the campaign against Israel?

Adonizedec (Joshua 10:3–4)

Puzzle 12

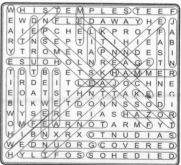

Which prophet ordered the
attack on Sisera's army?

Deborah (Judges 4:14)

Puzzle 13

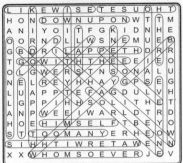

How many of Gideon's
men lapped up the water?

Three hundred (Judges 7:7)

Puzzle 14

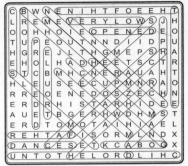

When did Jephthah surrender
his daughter to the Lord?

After two months (Judges 11:39)

Puzzle 15

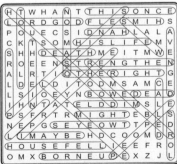

What two things did
the riddle stand for?

Honey and a lion (Judges 14:18)

Puzzle 16

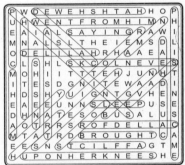

Who was the Israelite judge
with unusual strength?

Samson (Judges 16:6)

Puzzle 17

What special commitment did
Samson's strength come from?

The Nazarite vow (Judges 13:7)

Puzzle 18

Where did Naomi and Ruth live before
they traveled together to the land of Judah?

Moab (Ruth 1:1–4)

Puzzle 19

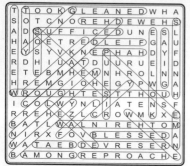

What country did Ruth
originate from?

Moab (Ruth 1:4)

Puzzle 20

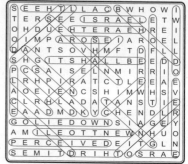

Who were the parents of this
miracle child named Samuel?

Elkanah and Hannah (1 Samuel 1:19)

Puzzle 21

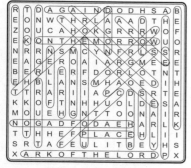

What carried the ark
home to the Israelites?

An oxen cart (1 Samuel 6:11–12)

Puzzle 22

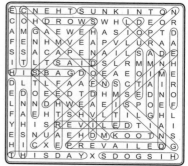

Where was the place Israel
faced the Philistines?

Shochoh (1 Samuel 17:1)

Puzzle 23

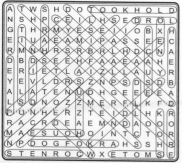

Whose house held the
ark for three months?

Obed-edom's (2 Samuel 6:11)

Puzzle 24

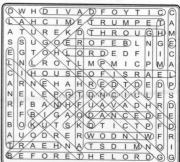

What resulted from
Michal's bad attitude?

She was barren (2 Samuel 6:23)

Puzzle 25

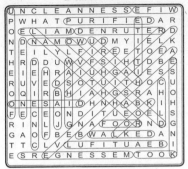

What army killed Uriah
during a battle?

The Ammonites (2 Samuel 11)

Puzzle 26

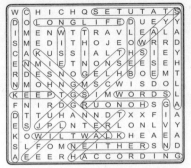

Which queen traveled to Jerusalem
to see Solomon's wisdom firsthand?

The queen of Sheba (1 Kings 10:1)

Puzzle 27

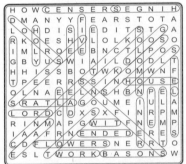

How many years total did it take Solomon
to build his own personal home?

Thirteen (1 Kings 7:1)

Puzzle 28

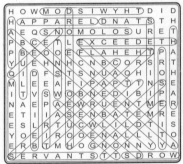

How did the queen of
Sheba test Solomon?

With hard questions (1 Kings 10:1)

Puzzle 29

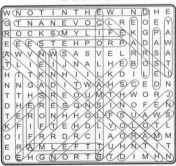

Where was Elijah hiding when the
word of the Lord came to him?

In a cave (1 Kings 19:9)

Puzzle 30

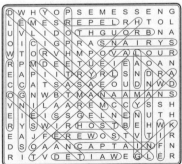

Whose messenger told Naaman
to wash in the Jordan River?

Elisha's (2 Kings 5:10)

Puzzle 31

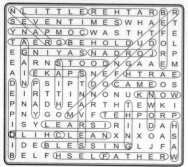

What was the leper Naaman's position
under the king of Syria?

Captain of the host (2 Kings 5:1)

Puzzle 32

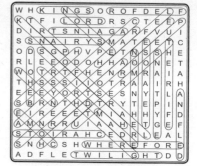

Who first discovered that
the Syrians had fled?

Four leprous men (2 Kings 7:3)

Puzzle 33

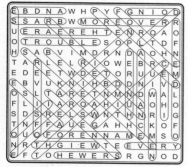

Why was David not allowed
to build a house for God?

He had shed much blood (1 Chronicles 22:8)

Puzzle 34

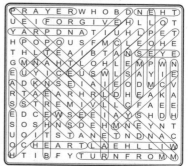

Who built the house that
God had chosen to sanctify?

Solomon (2 Chronicles 7:11)

Puzzle 35

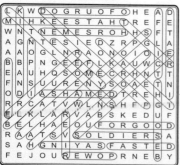

Where was Ezra going when
he asked for a safe journey?

To Jerusalem (Ezra 8:31)

Puzzle 36

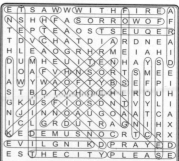

What post did Nehemiah
have with King Artaxerxes?

Cupbearer (Nehemiah 1:11)

Puzzle 37

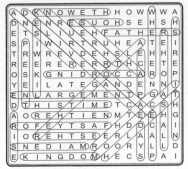

How was Esther related to Mordecai?

She was Mordecai's adopted daughter; the
daughter of Mordecai's uncle (Esther 2:7)

Puzzle 38

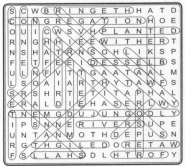

What personal possession did
King Ahasuerus give to Mordecai?

His ring (Esther 8:2)

Puzzle 39

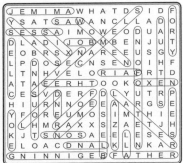

What did Satan claim would be Job's response if the
Lord took everything from him?

Satan claimed Job would curse
God to His face (Job 1:9–11)

Puzzle 40

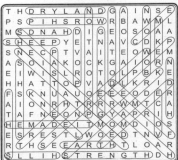

What does this psalm say
shall happen to the ungodly?

They shall perish (Psalm 1:6)

Puzzle 41

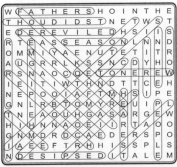

Who in the New Testament said
the opening words of this psalm?

Jesus (Matthew 27:46)

Puzzle 42

This psalm says to make what
kind of noise to the Lord?

A joyful noise (Psalm 95:1)

Puzzle 43

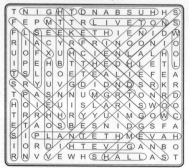

The price of a virtuous woman
is far above what?

Rubies (Proverbs 31:10)

Puzzle 44

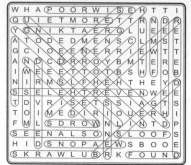

What title describes the
writer of this book?

The Preacher (Ecclesiastes 1:1)

Puzzle 45

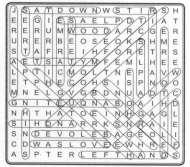

What rose is mentioned
in this chapter?

Rose of Sharon (Song of Songs 2:1)

Puzzle 46

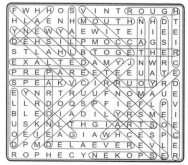

Who in the New Testament
fulfilled Isaiah's prophecy?

John the Baptist (Matthew 3:1–3)

Puzzle 47

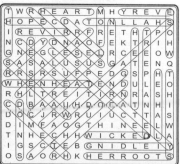

What king conquered
Judah in this book?

Nebuchadnezzar (Jeremiah 24:1)

Puzzle 48

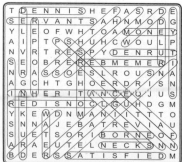

The army of what country brought
God's judgment on Jerusalem?

Babylon (Jeremiah 52:12–13)

Puzzle 49

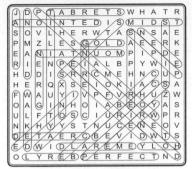

What river was Ezekiel by
when he saw his first vision?

The river Chebar (Ezekiel 1:3)

Puzzle 50

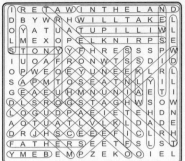

By what expression does
God address Ezekiel?

Son of man (Ezekiel 36:1)

Puzzle 51

What was the name of the
country the king ruled over?

Babylon (Daniel 1:1)

Puzzle 52

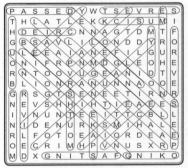

What king did Daniel
serve under after Darius?

Cyrus the Persian (Daniel 6:28)

Puzzle 53

What prostitute did the prophet Hosea marry to
picture God's relationship with faithless Israel?

Gomer (Hosea 1:3)

Puzzle 54

Which flying bug does Joel say is
part of God's judgment on Israel?

Locust (Joel 1:4)

Puzzle 55

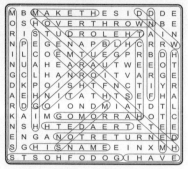

Besides being a prophet, what vocation did Amos engage in?

Herdman (Amos 1:1)

Puzzle 56

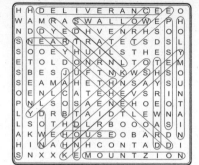

How many verses does the Old Testament's shortest book, Obadiah, contain?

Twenty-one

Puzzle 57

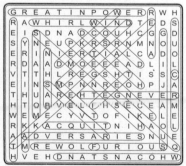

How many people lived in the city of Nineveh when Jonah preached in it?

Six-score thousand, that is, 120,000 (Jonah 4:11)

Puzzle 58

Which verse in Micah's prophecy names Bethlehem as the birthplace of Jesus?

Micah 5:2

Puzzle 59

What did Nahum call his prophecy of Nineveh?

"The burden" (Nahum 1:1)

Puzzle 60

How many chapters does the book of the prophet Habakkuk contain?

Three

Puzzle 61

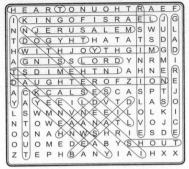

What Assyrian capital, well known to Jonah, is doomed by Zephaniah?

Nineveh (Zephaniah 2:13)

Puzzle 62

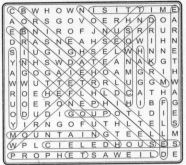

Who was governor of Judah when Haggai urged the rebuilding of the temple?

Zerubbabel (Haggai 1:1)

Puzzle 63

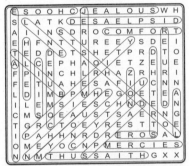

What kind of trees did the prophet Zechariah's angelic messenger stand among?

Myrtle (Zechariah 1:8)

Puzzle 64

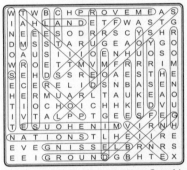

What was God's charge against Israel in Malachi chapter three, verse eight?

"Ye have robbed me" (Malachi 3:8)

Puzzle 65

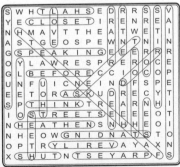

Where in Matthew's Gospel are specific instructions on how to pray?

Matthew 6:9–13

Puzzle 66

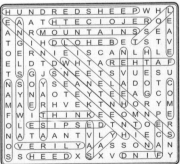

What are the stories called that Jesus used to teach very important lessons?

Parables (Matthew 13:3)

Puzzle 67

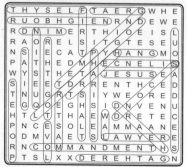

Where were the Israelites encamped when they were given the Ten Commandments?

Near Mount Sinai (Exodus 19)

Puzzle 68

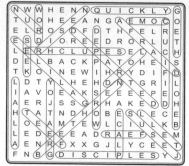

When the angel of the Lord rolled back the stone, why did the grave keepers shake and become like dead men?

"For fear of him" (Matthew 28:4)

Puzzle 69

Why could Jesus no longer enter a town openly after He healed a man with leprosy?

Because the man shared freely that Jesus had healed him (Mark 1:40–45)

Puzzle 70

What does the Lord promise will never pass away—even though heaven and earth will?

His Word (Mark 13:31)

Puzzle 71

Why did Jesus rebuke the disciples before He told them to preach the gospel?

For their lack of faith and unbelief that He was risen (Mark 16:14)

Puzzle 72

Who told Mary that her relative Elisabeth was expecting a child?

The angel Gabriel (Luke 1:26–36)

Puzzle 73

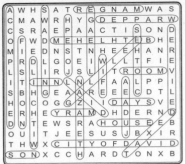

What was Mary's reaction when the angel first appeared to give her news about Jesus' birth?

She was troubled (Luke 1:29)

Puzzle 74

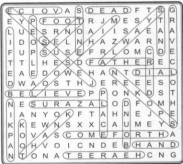

What did the shepherds do after they found Mary, Joseph, and the baby Jesus in the manger?

They spread the word to others about the birth of Jesus (Luke 2:17)

Puzzle 75

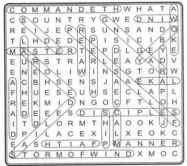

What country were Jesus and the disciples traveling to when Jesus' calming of the storm took place?

The country of the Gadarenes (Luke 8:26)

Puzzle 76

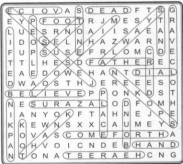

After Jesus raised Lazarus from the dead, what was the response of many of the Jews?

They believed in Jesus (John 11:45)

Puzzle 77

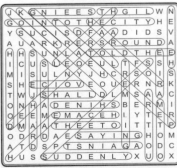

Why did Saul journey to Damascus?

To persecute Christians and bring them bound to Jerusalem (Acts 9:2)

Puzzle 78

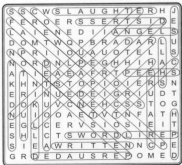

Where did Paul intend to go after visiting Rome?

Spain (Romans 15:24)

Puzzle 79

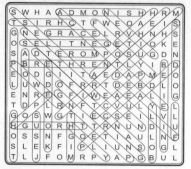

What work did Tertius fulfill for Paul?

He transcribed the epistle to the Romans
(Romans 16:22)

Puzzle 80

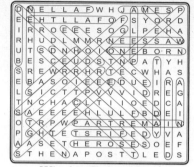

Why does Paul say he was
the least of the apostles?

He persecuted the church of God
(1 Corinthians 15:9)

Puzzle 81

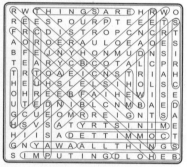

Who reported to Paul
about the Corinthians?

Titus (2 Corinthians 7:6–7)

Puzzle 82

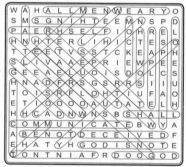

Whose Spirit cries out,
"Abba, Father"?

The Spirit of His Son (Galatians 4:6)

Puzzle 83

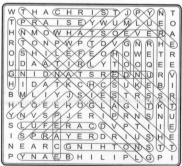

What number describes
faith, hope, and baptism?

One (Ephesians 4:5)

Puzzle 84

What woman prayed by the
riverside near Philippi?

Lydia (Acts 16:12–14)

Puzzle 85

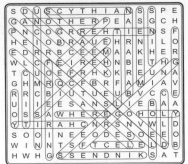

Speech should be with grace
seasoned with what?

Salt (Colossians 4:6)

Puzzle 86

Whose house in Thessalonica
was assaulted by a mob?

Jason's (Acts 17:1, 5)

Puzzle 87

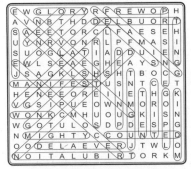

What does Paul say about
those who would not work?

Neither should they eat (2 Thessalonians 3:10)

Puzzle 88

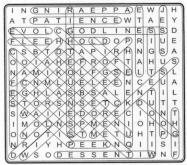

In what way does Paul call
Timothy his son?

Son in the faith (1 Timothy 1:2)

Puzzle 89

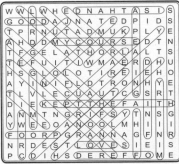

What did Paul tell Timothy
to let no man despise?

His (Timothy's) youth (1 Timothy 4:12)

Puzzle 90

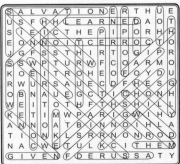

The father of Timothy was
of what nationality?

Greek (Acts 16:1)

Puzzle 91

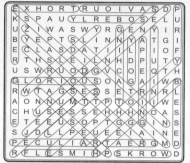

Paul was writing to Titus
who was on what island?

Crete (Titus 1:5)

Puzzle 92

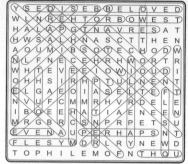

What was the name of the slave
being returned to Philemon?

Onesimus (Philemon 10)

Puzzle 93

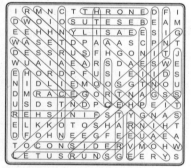

In time past, how did
God speak to the fathers?

By the prophets (Hebrews 1:1)

Puzzle 94

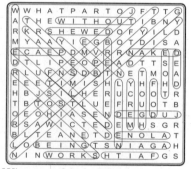

What part of the body is a little member
but boasts great things?

The tongue (James 3:5)

Puzzle 95

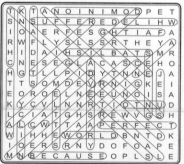

Peter says they are a holy nation
and what kind of people?

Peculiar (1 Peter 2:9)

Puzzle 96

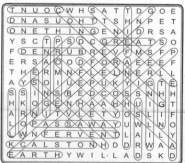

What does Peter say scoffers
of the last day will ask?

Where is the promise of His coming?
(2 Peter 3:3–4)

Puzzle 97

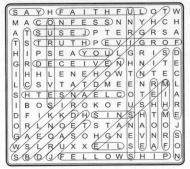

How many chapters appear in the New Testament book of First John?

Five

Puzzle 98

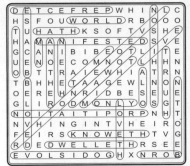

Which four books of the Bible contain the word "beginning" in their first verse?

Genesis, Mark, John, and 1 John

Puzzle 99

What two Old Testament cities are named in Jude's letter?

Sodom and Gomorrah (Jude 7)

Puzzle 100

What mythical creature appears in Revelation's twelfth chapter?

A dragon (Revelation 12:3)

Puzzle 101

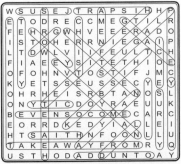

Who received the Revelation of Jesus Christ and recorded it for us today?

John (Revelation 1:1)

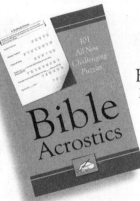
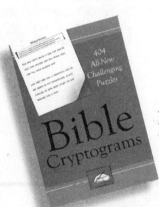